HOPE
IN ANY
CRISIS

BILL JOHNSON

CHARISMA
HOUSE

Most Charisma House Book Group products are available at special quantity discounts for bulk purchase for sales promotions, premiums, fund-raising, and educational needs. For details, call us at (407) 333-0600 or visit our website at www.charismahouse.com.

HOPE IN ANY CRISIS by Bill Johnson
Published by Charisma House
Charisma Media/Charisma House Book Group
600 Rinehart Road, Lake Mary, Florida 32746

This book or parts thereof may not be reproduced in any form, stored in a retrieval system, or transmitted in any form by any means—electronic, mechanical, photocopy, recording, or otherwise—without prior written permission of the publisher, except as provided by United States of America copyright law.

Unless otherwise noted, all Scripture quotations are taken from the New King James Version®. Copyright © 1982 by Thomas Nelson. Used by permission. All rights reserved.

Scripture quotations marked NASB are from the New American Standard Bible, copyright © 1960, 1962, 1963, 1968, 1971, 1972, 1973, 1975, 1977, 1995 by The Lockman Foundation. Used by permission. www.Lockman.org

All italics in Scripture quotations represent the author's emphasis.

Copyright © 2020 by Bill Johnson
All rights reserved

Visit the author's website at bjm.org.

HOPE
IN ANY
CRISIS

[signature]

Ps. 34:8

Rs. 34:8

Library of Congress Cataloging-in-Publication Data:
An application to register this book for cataloging has been
submitted to the Library of Congress.
International Standard Book Number: 978-1-62999-904-3
E-book ISBN: 978-1-62999-905-0

20 21 22 23 24 — 987654321
Printed in the United States of America

CONTENTS

INTRODUCTION

YOU MAY HAVE come to read this book because of a pandemic, natural disaster, or personal loss or devastation. Take heart; nothing catches God by surprise. On top of that, He has an answer to every earthly dilemma in His heart and mind right now. He is for us, and He longs to reveal His solutions to those who ask.

It would be wonderful if in writing this book, I could bring encouragement and hope to many. But if I'm honest, I want more than that. Much more. While I long to see people set free from fear or healed of their infirmities, I also want to see them bring that same liberty to others. In other words, I want the delivered to become deliverers, the blessed to become a blessing, and the comforted to become comforters.

Hopelessness is rooted in a lie, while hope is founded on the goodness of God. And yet both hope and hopelessness are contagious. We have to choose what is going to influence our hearts and minds and in doing so determine the kind of influence we're going to have on those around us.

The inspiration for this book came out of the unprecedented season of isolation and uncertainty caused by the spread of COVID-19. Both the disease and fear are pandemic, each with its own devastating consequences. But we are not left helpless victims to the whims of the powers of darkness. Jesus has given us solutions. And He has given us His authority. As you read this book, my prayer is that you will choose to embrace hope and then go out and infect as many others around you as you can.

In these pages you'll find comfort in the safety of abiding in God's presence, wisdom in three biblical responses to crisis, and power in returning to the basics of spending daily time in God's Word, prayer, and Communion. It doesn't matter what the situation is; you and I are always called to usher in the answer, which is the gospel of Jesus Christ. This is our privilege as believers.

CHAPTER ONE

LIVING IN HOPE IN A HOPELESS WORLD

WHEN JESUS DECLARED that the last days would be filled with war, famine, earthquakes, and other disasters, He wasn't trying to discourage those who follow Him. Instead, He was describing the conditions into which He was sending His last-days army. This might be a surprising way to start a book on hope, but I believe it's the approach we need to take. Hope isn't just a feeling we search for; it's something we grab hold of and bring into every situation in our lives.

We were created with promise and purpose, with the same responsibilities to illustrate the heart of the Father that Jesus modeled for us all. He said that if we believed in Him, we would do even greater works than He did.

> Most assuredly, I say to you, he who believes in Me, the works that I do he will do also; and greater works than these he will do, because I go to My

Father. And whatever you ask in My name, that I
will do, that the Father may be glorified in the Son.
—John 14:12–13

We often miss a key part of this promise: it was possible only because He was going to His Father. We have to ask what this has to do with our impossible-to-understand assignment. How does His return to the right hand of the Father affect our ability to do the works of the Father at the level set by Jesus, let alone beyond? Jesus explained this when He said that if He didn't go, the Holy Spirit would not be sent (John 16:7). The third person of the Trinity, the Holy Spirit, is the connection between what is seemingly impossible and the actual fulfillment of His promise.

After mentioning He was going to the Father, He promised He would do for us anything we asked. The easiest thing in the world to do with such an extreme promise is to try to water it down, mostly to make ourselves feel more comfortable in our current level of breakthrough in miracles. While I can't speak for you, I can speak for myself: I am not in this to feel comfortable. My heart is for Him to receive glory and for me to be like Jesus. That's it, pure and not so simple.

Let's take a look at the phrase "whatever you ask." Forget for just a moment that He just promised something beyond our wildest dreams and imaginations.

The part we can't afford to forget is the word *ask.* In other words, *prayer.* When Jesus gave us the command to pray for it to be "on earth as it is in heaven," it was first a commandment to pray (Matt. 6:9–10). This is the way of the kingdom of God.

We also know that both Jesus and the Holy Spirit are interceding for us before the Father.

> For we do not know what we should pray for as we ought, but *the Spirit Himself makes intercession for us* with groanings which cannot be uttered.
>
> —ROMANS 8:26

> It is *Christ* who died, and furthermore is also risen, who is even at the right hand of God, who *also makes intercession for us.*
>
> —ROMANS 8:34

Sandwiched between those two extraordinary gifts is a promise that is often quoted, "All things work together for good to those who love God" (Rom. 8:28). Both Jesus and the Holy Spirit are interceding for us. No wonder all things work for good. Prayer is the greatest place of influence, and the Son and the Spirit take their positions for our sake and illustrate our greatest call.

One of the things central to Jesus' lifestyle of purity and power was His prayer life. He spent time with His Father. This is stated throughout the four Gospels.

As we read through John 14–16, we find

overwhelming evidence that Jesus lived to see the Father glorified through all He said and did. For that reason, He said only what He heard His Father say and did only what He saw His Father do. He even stated that He would answer our anything-we-ask prayer for the Father's glory. It's amazing, really.

Maintaining Strength Through Hope

Maintaining personal strength in the midst of impossible circumstances is the right thing to do for our sake. It not only enables us to dwell in all that is stable in God Himself; it also helps us to become a resource to those under our influence. In a sense, this is our debt to the world: the ark of stability in unstable times.

Many virtues equip us to have influence during difficult times, but the one I look to the most often is hope. The measure of hope that I possess determines the measure of my influence.

When trouble strikes, people are so hungry for hope that they flock to those who have it. Often unbelievers are secure in their sin until shaking comes. They come face to face with their own vulnerabilities and consider the purpose of their lives. Being strong is necessary both for our sake and for the sake of others. It's also important for us to realize that both hope and hopelessness are contagious. We get to decide what we want to release to those around us.

I have a favorite way of defining *hope*: the joyful anticipation of good. This is the actual meaning of the biblical concept.[1] This is quite different from the common use of the word in our culture. Someone might say, "I sure hope that happens." That usage is the same as having a wish or a dream. It is far from absolute or guaranteed. The biblical concept of hope couldn't be more different from the common use in culture. Hope attracts what it anticipates.

I understand that some give the appearance of being hopeful, but in reality they are living in denial. In other words, their hope is unfounded and imaginary. It works hard to be unattached to reality. But that error doesn't erase the reality of the kingdom of God that is present and superior to every other reality on earth. This biblical kind of hope is anchored in that which is both unmovable and indestructible: the nature and promises of God.

Maintaining Strength Through Peace

To make it possible for us to follow in His footsteps, Jesus gave us another virtue: peace.

> Peace I leave with you, My peace I give to you; not as the world gives do I give to you. Let not your heart be troubled, neither let it be afraid.
>
> —JOHN 14:27

This peace is different from every other peace known to man. The world's definition of *peace* is always the absence of something: a time without war, a time without noise, or a time without conflict. The peace that He gives is in the form of a person. He is the Prince of Peace. He is our peace.

To truly benefit from that peace, we must do as He said. We cannot let our hearts be troubled. Nor can we let them be afraid. If we are afraid or troubled, it is because we have allowed ourselves to be; we have given anxiety permission to steal our awareness of the Prince of Peace, who will never leave or forsake us. Guilt and shame won't help, but taking responsibility for what we've allowed into our hearts is a good first step to freedom.

Discovering What's Within Reach

How easy it is to become overwhelmed with personal problems, let alone pandemic diseases, economic disruptions, and political unrest. And yet the kingdom of God is real and present. Jesus tells us that the kingdom of God is at hand (Mark 1:15). Another way to put it is the kingdom is in the here and now; it's within reach.

Jesus modeled this beautifully when He slept in the storm, and He is our example who can and must be followed. He was able to sleep in the storm because the world He dwells in has no storms. Period. He modeled living from heaven to earth. He showed us what it was like to dwell in heavenly places before the apostle Paul found language for it in Ephesians:

> But God, who is rich in mercy, because of His great love with which He loved us, even when we were dead in trespasses, made us alive together with Christ (by grace you have been saved), and raised us up together, and *made us sit together in the heavenly places in Christ Jesus.*
>
> —EPHESIANS 2:4–6

The point is, this reality is far too great to keep as a belief that is unaccompanied by experience. To be truly seated in heavenly places in Christ must be measurable by the change in perspective and thinking that has occurred in my life.

Revelation of biblical truth is an invitation to experience that truth. For example, God would never reveal Himself as a Savior merely to increase our spiritual intelligence. He shows us who He is as our Savior that we might experience His salvation. This knowledge of salvation is of little benefit if it is not accompanied by the salvation He promises. In the same way, He doesn't enable us to see Him as our provider to make us smarter. He does it so that our hearts will be opened to experience and trust Him for His provision in the daily parts of our lives.

Being seated in heavenly places is a wonderful truth, but it must be accompanied by experience for its purpose to be fully realized. We know that the seated-in-heavenly-places promise has become our own experience when we see and think differently. We see from His perspective, and the mind of Christ becomes our norm. This is the ongoing challenge of every believer that we must constantly affirm.

Biblical meditation is probably one of the most forgotten biblical disciplines. And yet it is here that these wonderful truths of Scripture take root deeper than the lies given to us by the culture that surrounds us. Eastern meditation is different in that it requires its practitioners to empty their minds. That is dangerous, as there are many powers that look for vacated places to fill. Biblical meditation is where we fill our minds with truth and bring it up over and over again for consideration. The word *meditate* can be translated "to mutter,"[2] which speaks of our willingness to repeat a truth over and over to ourselves. Oftentimes in that journey, the Lord adds to our understanding until that truth becomes a part of our character, our personality. As some would say, truth becomes cellular. It becomes who we are.

Worldview vs. God View

Our worldview is always shaped by our view of God. Who is He? What is He like? What has He designed us to be? The answers to questions like these determine what we expect to happen in our lifetime and how we should then live. Our view of God is not merely philosophical. It is the reality from which we choose to live.

For me, the goodness of God is the most nonnegotiable thing in my life. It is the cornerstone of my theology. Interestingly, understanding this truth began to dramatically increase in my life after the loss of my dad through disease. That might seem like an odd time to learn such a thing. But in reality I can't think of a better time to learn it than when we're in the middle of circumstances that war against the knowledge of God in our hearts. With the goodness of God in place, everything else is subject to that primary truth.

> The LORD is good, a stronghold in the day of trouble; and He knows those who trust in Him.
> —NAHUM 1:7

His goodness is best seen in times of trouble. This becomes a place of refuge for the whole person— spirit, soul, and body. To the Lord, trust is always the central issue. He knows those who trust Him. But no matter how wonderful the subject of goodness is, that goodness is not defined by the surrounding culture. It is illustrated in the person of Jesus Christ, who healed everyone who came to Him but also chased the money changers out of the temple with a whip. He astonished people with His insights as He taught them how to live, but He was also silent before Pilate, unwilling to answer his questions. All His actions come from His goodness, revealing what He values and is willing to protect.

When things look out of control on a personal level or even in an international conflict, I return to the place of great safety and promise: the goodness of God. It repels the confusing thoughts and the bent toward embracing inferior answers or solutions. Remember, the enemy is not just trying to get me to sin. He is satisfied whenever I embrace an inferior way of thinking and compromised purpose for my life. He wants me outside what I was designed for. But when I anchor my heart in the goodness of God, I become cemented in the reality of His personhood and live from that place of supernatural peace. For me that is sanity in a sometimes insane world.

Many people can recite the correct biblical answer for a problem, but the truth they speak of has little effect on their emotions or thought life. These truths, which are the greatest of all realities, must become a part of us. That means that while having biblical answers is a good start, it is not the finish line. The mind of Christ is never manipulated or controlled by fear. It is never bound by unbelief or stifled by human limitation. It consistently ushers in heaven's solutions for earthly dilemmas.

Feeding the Heart and Mind

My wife and I love to work out, especially lifting weights. In this season of my life, almost all my workouts are in the morning. But when I started around thirty years ago, my workouts were all late in the afternoon. I noticed something I didn't expect: my strength and endurance were affected by what I ate for lunch. It was quite surprising to me but true. If I ate a healthy meal, I was stronger. If I didn't, my workout suffered. When I started realizing this fact, I began to eat for my workout. Food then became a power source, and I gained some wisdom. I suppose it wouldn't have mattered if my time in the gym weren't important to me. But it was. As a result, food had become fuel. Its purpose was beyond personal pleasure. This new experience meant I mentally began my workout hours before I got to the gym by choosing well what I should eat.

Likewise, the way we feed ourselves emotionally, intellectually, and spiritually has a great effect on the strength that sustains us. Such strength ultimately positions us to bring transformation to the world around us.

We are the most overfed culture ever to walk the earth. The media serves to provide us with information and input even beyond the dreams of any prior generation. I love it in all its various forms. But without wisdom, discernment, and intentionality with the use of our time, what is supposed to serve us becomes our master. Never is this more obvious than in a national or world crisis. The mainstream media takes center stage in homes all around the world.

Let me first say I'm thankful for those who work so hard to keep us informed with world events. Many wonderful people serve selflessly that we might live intelligently and successfully. The news services of the world offer us a luxury that was not afforded in prior generations in the same measure that it is today. And sometimes these reporters even put themselves at great risk to bring us a story. Honor is due. And yet this luxury has become our undoing. One can receive more bad news in a day than previous generations would have in a year or more. As I recently told our Bethel Church family, "If your input from mainstream media is greater than your input from the Word of God, your discouragement is self-inflicted."

The worldview of the reporter, and more importantly the worldview of the management of the news outlet, determines what and how something will be reported. There is bias. And sometimes there is downright deception. Rarely are news outlets held accountable for the deception in their reports. "The end justifies the means" becomes the mantra of the day, as their intention of controlling and shaping culture to their ideals becomes valued over truth itself. Overall the ideals of the media giants are liberal and godless. We must pray for righteousness and truth to prevail in all places of influence in our world. Thankfully there are more and more righteous people in all realms of society, including the media. I pray for their spiritual safety and promotion.

The point is, we must take responsibility for our emotional and intellectual intake. We must resist anything that competes in our hearts with our awareness of our Father, who has answers for every problem. All the solutions for life are in His heart right now, and believers have legal access to these things. They are called mysteries and are a part of our spiritual inheritance. But if I become more aware of the work of the enemy than I am of the presence and nature of God, I will live in reaction to the devil. Jesus didn't live that way. He lived in response to the Father. And He is the One I follow. The devil is not worthy of any influence in my life, even if I were to live in reaction, attempting to destroy his works. Responding to our heavenly Father positions me to be a part of the solution. That is the way of Jesus and must become the way of all who follow.

Let's be honest: fear sells. One needs only to look at the fear caused by the potential problem with Y2K, only twenty-some years ago. Incredible numbers of generators and other survival goods were sold to people who wanted to be wise and be prepared.

Fear makes a news program popular or a print media outlet valued. It also serves the media by making the advertisement space on TV or the columns of the newspaper or magazine of greater value. The point is, our media outlets often become brokers of fear just to keep the bills paid. The only reason it is accepted in our culture is that it masquerades as wisdom. We have changed from a people who value responsibilities to a people who worship personal rights. Whenever rights are exalted over responsibility, disaster is the only possible outcome. A steady diet of continual disasters will eventually reduce me to a person who wants the return of Christ not because of love but because of my desire to escape.

As a result, the most fearful among us think they're the most informed. Eating from the tree of the knowledge of good and evil does not make one wise. It becomes the poison of the soul, leading to resistance to the purposes of God. Unbelief is the end result of selling our souls to fear, which is obviously forbidden in Scripture.

Tragic conditions such as the COVID-19 pandemic, the economy, or conflict in the Middle East have answers and solutions. The world system wants us to stay dependent on the media for bad news until the next problem arises. Avoid such nonsense at all costs.

The heart and mind reveal quite quickly what they have been feeding on. The strength for the workout called faith is quick to show whether I've been feeding my heart on the Word of God, which reveals His heart, or on the hopeless condition of the world I'm called to change. Hope will always be in the heart of the one who feasts liberally on the heart and promises of our perfect heavenly Father.

Bound by Design

Our purpose is revealed in our design. But whenever society removes the concept of a creator from its consciousness, it creates liberties we were never designed for—which actually work to destroy us. Once the designer is removed, so is design. You can't have design without a designer. When our design is gone, our intended purpose is undermined. When purpose is removed, so is our destiny. When we have no God-given destiny, we have no need for accountability, which destroys all that's left of the fear of God, the beginning of wisdom. This helps to explain the erosion of society where if a man feels like a woman, he has the right to choose to be one. Such nonsense is logical only when the boundaries of design are ignored.

We find that we were created in the image of God

Himself. That is a stunning design, revealing a purpose that is beyond our capacity to dream of for ourselves. Whenever we remove the idea of being created in the image of God, we lose the value of human life. Abortion testifies to this tragedy, as do many other similar atrocities. The absolutes must be held in place. They serve as anchors in turbulent waters. Without them we are at the mercy of every whim and fancy of what's popular in culture at the moment.

The boundaries set by our design are restrictions. But all God's restrictions are for the purpose of increased life. None of them are punishments. They are avenues of liberty, discovered identity, and increase. They result in the greater freedoms and experiences of life we were all made to delight in. A no in one part of life is a yes to another part of life. He is a life giver! His restrictions are to keep us from the things that steal, kill, and destroy.

Think of it as the double yellow line painted down the center of the road on a two-lane highway. Cars traveling in opposite directions at fifty-five miles per hour come within a few feet of each other countless times. This happens day after day with no problems. But without the restriction created by that painted line, there would be certain death and suffering for countless numbers of people. Yet because of the restriction created by the lines, we get to our destinations safely. God's restrictions are guidelines for safety but also ultimately for enjoyment. He created all things for His delight and for our pleasure.

The Irreverence of Hope

We were designed with purpose and destiny. Survival is important but is inferior as a lifetime goal. We were designed to soar. Managing our intake of information that fuels our purpose is real wisdom.

The thought of soaring during times of crisis almost seems flippant to many. Yet trials don't affect our destinies. They affect only the journey. And considering that our Father is the One who uses all things for His glory and our strength, we must hold on to hope. Even the most undesirable situation can be used for our promotion.

Deliberately feeding ourselves on the things that make us useful in crises is paramount to our fulfilling our design. We were born to live and thrive with hope!

Hope is the soil that faith grows in. Hope doesn't cower in the face of a mountain, but it is faith that removes the mountain. Hope is a general approach to all things in life. Faith is specific and intentional. Faith is not the result of striving. It is the result of surrender. Yielding to the purposes of God and, more specifically, to the Word of God is the pathway of great hope and faith.

Hope has to have a foundation. And that foundation is the goodness of God. A person without hope either has lost sight of His goodness or was never convinced in the first place. Regardless, the solution is simple: Return to Him. Return to the One who loves us beyond measure. It doesn't get any simpler or more profound than this.

> For God so loved the world that He gave His only begotten Son, that whoever believes in Him should not perish but have everlasting life.
>
> —JOHN 3:16

That is pure, unadulterated goodness. Paul adds to this truth:

> He who did not spare His own Son, but delivered Him up for us all, how shall He not with Him also freely give us all things?
>
> —ROMANS 8:32

His gift to us was so extreme that everything else needed in this life, and throughout all eternity, was automatically included. Meditating on such truths should give us the courage and hope to approach life with certainty. It's not a certainty of knowing what will happen and when. It's a certainty that we are held in His hand and are automatically positioned for forward motion and increase.

Rereading the Love Letter

The Word of God brings life. Not to fill our hearts with this beautiful gift from heaven is to live within reach of water yet see how long we can go without a drink. It is foolish.

Whenever I face something that challenges my faith, whether it's personal or extreme such as a pandemic, I return to the Word of God to find out what He has to say. I also review the prophetic words spoken over our lives to see if there might be something with which to feed my soul. This has become my lifestyle for so long that I don't even have to think about doing it. It is automatic.

When our city was devastated by the Carr Fire in 2018, I was in England. I got on a plane the next day to fly home. I spent much of that flight reviewing the Word of God to find strength and insight so that I could become a voice of hope for a church and city under devastation.

When I got home, Redding looked like a war zone in every possible way. Death, loss, and destruction were everywhere. But God's Word remained true. And I can honestly say that Redding is at a better place of hope and promise than before the fires. Only God can do that.

Not only do I quickly turn to the Word of God in crisis, but I specifically go to the psalms. Most every emotion in life is found in that book. I read until I find my voice, my cry, on the pages of Scripture. When I do, I know that I am in a place to hear and learn the heart of God for me and my future. I owe my immediate family, my church family, and my community a heart filled with hope. And even if it seems impossible, I must at least be headed in that direction. In the next chapter, I want to address this question: What do I do if I'm feeling overwhelmed, hopeless, and weak?

CHAPTER TWO

HELP! I LOST MY PEACE

WE OFTEN PRAY for things we already have. Peace is a great example. Jesus told us He gave us peace that was different from and superior to any kind of peace you could get in the world. So if He gave it to me, why can't I find it? First of all, let's be clear: God didn't take the peace back. So then, peace is still given to me, but it's not a felt reality.

I'm not talking about basing our walk with Jesus on our emotions. They are unstable. Sometimes I'm up, and sometimes I'm down. But let's not reject this reality of emotions because we're afraid of becoming governed by them. Reaction to error almost always leads to another error, one that is culturally more acceptable in our environment. But it doesn't mean we're standing on truth. The apostle Paul makes a clarifying statement for us:

> For the kingdom of God is not eating and
> drinking, but righteousness and peace and joy in
> the Holy Spirit.
>
> —ROMANS 14:17

Righteousness, peace, and joy are manifestations of the kingdom of God, giving evidence of its impact on our lives in the here and now. They are the realms that describe the Holy Spirit's impact on a life. They are summed up in another verse as liberty or freedom: "Now the Lord is the Spirit; and where the Spirit of the Lord is, there is liberty" (2 Cor. 3:17). Wherever the lordship of Jesus is manifested, freedom is the evidence. Of the three manifestations of the kingdom mentioned in Romans 14, two are felt realities: peace and joy.

We know from Scripture that our salvation was to include forgiveness of sin, healing of disease, and deliverance from the torment of the evil one. All three realities were given to us in salvation; they are included in the meaning of the word for *salvation* in the original language. The word is *sozo*.[1] And so we see that this kingdom solves the issues of deficiency in our lives. Righteousness addresses the sin issue. Peace speaks to the issue of torment. And joy confronts the problem of sickness and disease. (Laughter is good medicine. See Proverbs 17:22.) All three were given to us in the kingdom, which is the realm of His dominion. In the same way that torment from demons cannot exist in heaven, it cannot exist wherever Jesus is Lord.

Feelings vs. Reality

So then, here we stand before one of our most significant challenges. If two-thirds of the kingdom of God in our lives is a felt reality, how come I don't feel forgiven? Does that mean I'm not really forgiven, because I don't feel as though I am? Absolutely not. As we learn to embrace with our yielded hearts the reality of Scripture, those realities become realized and felt.

For example, I have not been washed by the blood of Jesus and delivered from sin because I feel as though I have. Truly I have been because the Word of God says so. I have come to God in complete abandonment and have confessed my sin to Him, which basically means I agree with Him about the things He points to in my life, admitting they were wrong. The Bible says I'm forgiven. "If we confess our sins, He is faithful and just to forgive us our sins and to cleanse us from all unrighteousness" (1 John 1:9). Putting my faith in the Word of God results in forgiveness becoming a felt reality. The Word of God always reigns over my feelings. And as I become spiritually mature, being anchored in what God has said has a greater and greater effect over my emotions.

But What About My Peace?

Jesus declared that He gave us His peace. This implies that the problem of the lack of peace in a given situation is not on God's end of the equation; it's on ours. We have the responsibility to steward well all that He has given us. The Scripture goes on to say that His gifts are irrevocable, which means He doesn't take them back. (See Romans 11:29.) They remain ours.

I like to use a banking analogy for this: there's a difference between what's in my account and what's in my possession. In the natural I can starve to death because I have no food yet have millions of dollars in the bank. Learning to make withdrawals and stewarding those withdrawals well is the challenge that is often overlooked in our walk with Christ. To do this well, we must know what the Bible says about our salvation and become increasingly aware of that reality over everything that would contradict it. The Word of God takes precedence over every other word. Facing disasters of any kind requires that I learn this well, or I tragically become a victim when I was designed to be a victor.

Whenever I find myself without peace, I ask myself this question: Where did I leave it? First of all, let me say that peace is normal in my life. I'd never say that I do this perfectly, as that wouldn't be true. But over the years, I have learned to protect what I value most, which is His presence in my life. That means I guard the measure of peace (presence) He has allowed me to be aware of. Good stewardship of what we have is what gives us access to more.

Back to the question "Where did I leave my peace?" This is my typical response: I review the last few hours to see if I did something to grieve Him. Remember, He will not take peace out of my life. Peace is the result of "I am with you always" (Matt. 28:20). Sometimes in those moments of reflection, the Holy Spirit helps me to see what happened.

You can always tell when it's the Holy Spirit who points to a sin in attitude, action, or intent because He always brings hope. The enemy of our souls simply accuses until we mistakenly look at our mistake as our new identity. He brings hopelessness.

It may be the phone call I got early in the morning. As I look back, I can see that I became angry with a friend for something said or done. In that moment of discovery I genuinely repent for my poor stewardship of my heart and thus His priceless gift called peace. I then pray, "Father, forgive me. I embraced anger instead of Your peace. I receive the gift I could never earn, which is Your forgiveness. And according to Scripture, I embrace Your gift of peace once again."

Perhaps I watched a newscast about a pandemic or a mass shooting and became fearful. There is a healthy fear. That kind of fear keeps me from putting my hand on a hot stove. The wrong kind of fear tells me I can never use the stove because of its potential danger. The wrong kind of fear is seen in its hopelessness. The right kind of fear leads to biblical wisdom, which begins as the fear of God.

Courage and Faith Are Friends

Several things are important to know about faith in the face of crisis or disaster. First of all, it's impossible to please God apart from faith:

> But without faith it is impossible to please Him.
> —Hebrews 11:6

Second, He has made it possible for everyone to enter this great favor because He gave each person a measure of faith:

> God has dealt to each one a measure of faith.
> —Romans 12:3

Third, we are responsible for increasing what He has given us. This concept is borne true through the story of the talents (a sum of money) described in Matthew 25:14–30. Each of us has been given something to steward. Increase is always expected, as God has made this possible through our correct stewardship of whatever we've been given. In this example, the subject is faith. Simply put, faith grows with proper use. Much like a muscle, it grows with exercise.

Many make a mistake here and think that to move in faith means to have no doubts. As someone once said, "Faith is not the absence of doubt; it's the presence of belief." And as the father of the tormented child said to Jesus, "Lord, I believe; help my unbelief!" (Mark 9:24). It's OK to be in that condition. It's not OK to stay there.

Let's say I have a seemingly impossible situation before me. What do I do? It could be personal. It could be international. But my heart's response is to be the same. First of all, understanding is not needed for faith to function well, as faith does not come from the mind. When understanding is an expression of the renewed mind, it becomes like the banks of the river for faith to flow in. Perhaps this is oversimplified, but at a foundational level I am to embrace fear or love. I realize that my subject here is faith, but Galatians 5:6 says that faith works through love. They are two sides of the same coin. To embrace love/faith, I'll have to let go of fear. Besides, the problem I face is impossible only to the degree I remove God from the equation.

Pick Up the Right Sword

The Word of God cannot be overemphasized. It can be misused and abused, but it cannot be overemphasized.

Picking up the sword, which is the Word of God (Eph. 6:17), is vital in the battle over our thoughts. Victory in the battleground of the mind positions us for a break-through in the seemingly impossible situation—at least to the point where I am no longer a victim but instead function from the victory Jesus bought for me. In my personal life I return to my ministry to Him through thanksgiving, praise, and worship.

I realize some situations require immediate action, such as being involved in an accident. In that situation there is no time to quiet our hearts enough to be aware of His. This is where developing a heart of worship and the lifestyle of praying without ceasing comes into play. We then become "ready in season and out" (2 Tim. 4:2). And in that context we are ready for imme-diate action.

But let's return for a moment to my personal response. I worship not to manipulate Him, but to become more fully aware of Him who is with me always. And in that posture I'm more prone to discover His heart for that situation.

The Word of God, which is the sword of the Spirit, belongs in my heart and mind. If it is, I will have a clearer understanding of how to put it in my hand, meaning how to apply it to the immediate circum-stance through deliberate action. This is where I return to previous places in Scripture where God has met me in the past. I review to see if anything He has already highlighted would help me now. I also take time to read, especially through the psalms, until something speaks to me about the current situation.

There are three important things for me to discover when possible:

1. My heart condition must become anchored in absolute trust in God.

2. I must find what God is requiring of me. I must come to understand what is to be my response to the problem. This is where I receive practical instruction from God about my role.

3. I must discover God's intended outcome to the crisis. I never blame Him for earthquakes, pandemics, and the like. The devil came to steal, kill, and destroy. So as best as I can, I approach the given problem with the momentum that Jesus created for us in the Gospels. Once again, Jesus Christ is perfect theology. I must use His example to help me find the Father's heart for my current challenge.

How to Use the Sword

Many still seem to think our battle is against people because their continual use of the sword of the Spirit is to wield it against those with whom they disagree. We've often made a mess in the body of Christ simply because of our disregard of other members.

Perhaps this is what Paul was addressing when he spoke of Communion in this way: "For he who eats and drinks in an unworthy manner eats and drinks judgment to himself, *not discerning the Lord's body*. For this reason, many are weak and sick among you, and many sleep" (1 Cor. 11:29–30). We know the body is the bread we hold in our hands. But in the context of the instruction of these chapters, it must also mean His body, the church. "For *we, though many, are one bread and one body*; for we all partake of that one bread" (1 Cor. 10:17). I'll discuss more about Communion later in this book. The point here is, this sword is a weapon to be used against the enemy of our souls.

My first response to what God is speaking to my heart is to acknowledge that what He said is true and receive it deep into my heart. I can tell when I've done this successfully because my perspective begins to change, as do my thoughts about the problem. The Word of God takes root in my heart the more I meditate on what He has said. This means to repeatedly review His Word in my heart and mind until it becomes a part of me. My heart will always respond with conviction to anything God has said. That burning heart shows me that the Word is taking root in the deep part of my heart.

Secondly, we must respond with obedience to what He has said. Never does He speak for our entertainment. Our lives can be summed up with these words: we hear and obey. This is who we are—a people God has called to life with His voice that we might demonstrate that life to a planet in chaos. He called, we responded, and now we represent Him. Our response of obedience is varied, according to the word given. But let me generalize our response to three things: an act of faith, a prophetic act, and a decree.

Act of Faith

Faith requires an action to reveal its authenticity. Or, as James puts it, "Thus also faith by itself, if it does not have works, is dead" (Jas. 2:17). We all know of people who have done dumb things, supposedly from faith, that ended in disaster. Presumptuous acts are not real faith. These usually happen when someone is trying to prove he or she has great faith. Real faith doesn't need to prove itself or draw attention to itself. But by nature it demands expression. For some reason, the fear of getting it wrong often keeps us from getting it right.

James goes on to say of Abraham, considered the father of faith, "Do you see that faith was working together with his works, and by works faith was made perfect?" (v. 22). Faith "made perfect" means made mature or complete.[2] It's kind of like two-part epoxy. As long as the resin and hardener stay in their individual containers or are poured out by themselves and not blended together, nothing will be glued. It doesn't work. It requires the two parts to work together to have its intended effect. So faith exists in the heart that becomes solidified through action. It then becomes complete.

Action is required once God has spoken. For example, at times when I have been in desperate need of provision, He has led me to give whatever amount of money I did have away. The miracle of provision followed. The gift I gave could be considered seed for the harvest I was needing.

I also remember many times praying for a miracle of healing for someone that required an act of faith. In one situation a man had a seriously injured foot and was in great need of a miracle. He was actually on his way to the hospital but asked his wife to bring him by our service. They arrived as we were dismissed and were leaving the building. I laid hands on him gently and prayed and prayed, and nothing happened. But then I sensed a direction from the Lord. I told him to slowly put weight on it. He did. And it was healed right before our eyes. We actually saw it happen.

The point is, faith needs an action. Ask Him what to do. By the way, I never evaluate whether I have enough faith for a situation. I can always obey. And that's all the faith that I need.

Prophetic Act

The prophetic act is quite different from the act of faith in that the action is unrelated to the intended outcome. With an act of faith I may put weight on the foot that needs healing. Both are acts of obedience, but that's where their similarity ends.

The Bible is full of stories with prophetic acts. Here are a couple that illustrate the point beautifully. The first story is about the sons of the prophets who borrowed an ax to help them build housing for their group. As they were cutting down a tree by the river, the ax-head flew off into the water. They were quite concerned, as it was borrowed and they had no money to pay the owner for a replacement. They came to Elisha with the problem. He asked where it fell in the water. "So the man of God said, 'Where did it fall?' And he showed him the place. So he cut off a stick, and threw it in there; and he made the iron float" (2 Kings 6:6). We can throw sticks into the water all day long, and we'll never get an ax-head to swim, as the action is in no way linked to the intended outcome. It was an unrelated action to the desired outcome that released the power of God.

The second example is the time when Jesus had a blind man go to the pool of Siloam. "A Man called Jesus made clay and anointed my eyes and said to me, 'Go to the pool of Siloam and wash.' So I went and washed, and I received sight" (John 9:11). There is no healing in those waters. In fact, it almost seems cruel to make a blind man go anywhere. And yet He did, as we can safely assume that is what the Father was doing. The blind man washed the mud from his eyes and was healed. The act of obedience that seemed unreasonable to everyone but the one in need brought the intended miracle.

Decree

Over time many things that were supposed to happen have never happened simply because they were never spoken. I don't mean to imply that our word is equal to God's. That would be foolish. But how powerful is God's word in a given moment when it is spoken by us? The word doesn't lose power because of the vessel it flows through. The word of the Lord for a given situation is still the word of the Lord. It has all the backing of heaven, but it must first be declared.

At times this can be as simple as a quiet confession that we make to ourselves. It can also be something declared in a public setting, much like a prophetic word. It can also be boldly declared even when you're not in a crowd. Many times I've sensed that God wanted to do something, and I've gone outside my home or office and made the decree out loud. In fact, sometimes I drive through the rougher parts of town and declare the word of the Lord over them.

Things of this nature must be declared. And sometimes it must be loud and forceful. Not because the spiritual realm is deaf. It's because we need to be all in, and forceful decrees of this nature put a demand on us. This is essential as we learn to express faith. This includes the bold decree of the gospel. Two of my favorite passages in this regard follow.

> Now, Lord, look on their threats and grant to Your servants that with all boldness they may speak Your word, by stretching out Your hand to heal, and that signs and wonders may be done through the name of Your holy Servant Jesus.
>
> —Acts 4:29–30

> And they went out and preached everywhere, the Lord working with them and confirming the word through the accompanying signs. Amen.
>
> —Mark 16:20

In both instances, we see miracles and healings as heaven's response to the bold preaching of the Word. We must not reduce this to what takes place behind traditional pulpits. This is referring to the declaration of truth in whatever setting we find ourselves.

There is also an important personal application of this wonderful truth. The Bible says, "Let the weak say, 'I am strong'" (Joel 3:10). Many times we become overwhelmed by the circumstances we are facing and consider ourselves weak. That is not a position of humility. It is a denial of reality—the reality that the blood of Jesus has qualified us for every victory that the cross and the resurrection of Jesus afforded us. If you're in that place, turn to Jesus and do what was commanded in Joel. Let the weak say, "I am strong!" Feeling strong has nothing to do with our strength. It is a fact in Christ, where we abide, and it must be spoken.

This principle comes with a warning. This is not a Christian trick that we use to get what we want out of life. It is a precious tool that is to be used to help bring about all that God intended when He assigned us the privilege of being alive during a crisis. This instrument is powerful for good or for bad. Proverbs, the book of wisdom, says, "Death and life are in the power of the tongue, and those who love it will eat its fruit" (18:21). This is not talking about making prophetic decrees; it is referring to our speech in general. We must hold ourselves accountable for how we speak and what we say.

Many times I've watched people undermine the miracle they were pursuing. Sometimes it goes like this: They need a miracle from God. So we pray together. Almost every time I finish praying for people, I ask them how they're doing. I want them to examine themselves to see what God has done. Only around 50 percent of the people we see healed actually feel it happen. That means the other half are clueless until they move in a way they couldn't without pain or restricted movement or in some way discover what God has done for them. Occasionally the moment I finish the prayer, the person will say, "I know He can do it!" Translated, he or she has just said, "I know He hasn't done it." It may be hard to describe on paper, but occasionally I can feel the power of those words. It's like pulling the plug on an electric appliance. It all stops. (Just to clarify, at times the power of God is so powerful that no one could stop what is happening through careless words.)

In the next chapter I want to take you on a journey, a personal journey, through a portion of Scripture that has taken center stage in this recent health crisis: Psalm 91. We will read it, pray it, and declare it together. Psalm 91 is the will of God.

Each of us being in a place of great strength in crisis not only is possible but is also God's heart for us all. There's no shame for anyone feeling lost in this challenging time. While there's no shame, there is an invitation. It's an invitation to God's faith, God's strength.

Jesus gave us a secret to His strength when He said, "My food is to do the will of Him who sent Me, and to finish His work" (John 4:34). We normally think of someone being fed by reading the Scriptures, which would be absolutely true. But He demonstrates a lesson here that is vital for all of us.

First, we must ask the question "What is food to our bodies?" Dining creates a time for fellowship and intimacy with those we love. Eating nourishes and strengthens us. Jesus was declaring that obeying the Father, whom He loved dearly, nourished and strengthened Him.

Many who consider themselves weak are essentially one action away from increased personal strength. That action may be providing food for those in need. It may be volunteering at the local hospital or making a list of needs and taking an hour or so to bring them before the Father. This list is endless. The point is, constantly thinking about problems would drain any of us. But doing something about them, no matter how trivial the action may seem, brings strength to us all. And we all need greater strength so we can be useful in representing King Jesus before a bewildered world.

Prepare yourself now to experience the beauty of Psalm 91.

CHAPTER THREE

PRAYING SOLUTIONS

THERE IS A sad reality for many people when it comes to the subject of prayer: sometimes people pray just to be able to say they've prayed. All too frequently, we pray without expecting an answer, but we learn to live with our conscience eased because we embraced the discipline of prayer. We were designed for answers. In fact, the design of the Lord for each one of us is that our breakthroughs in response to prayer would lead us into the *fullness of joy*! Jesus put it this way in John 16:24: "Ask, and you will receive, that your joy may be full." We owe answers to prayer to ourselves, to the world around us, and to God Himself. In the answer to prayer He is glorified and we overflow with a joyful life. We were designed for difficulty because we were given a secret weapon: answers to prayer.

The Word of God is both the rock of reason and the life source for all things supernatural. Read it, pray it, declare it, and enjoy it! It is a priceless gift from God.

While many will twist its meaning to justify their life-styles, it remains the same. Neither circumstance nor culture has the authority to change Scripture. When believed, it has the power to change both circumstances and cultures. The Word of God is the plumb line of reason and establishes the values needed for a successful life here on earth.

Again, look to God's Word when trials and impossibilities come your way. We must find out what God is saying in His Word. We must turn our attention to Him that we might contribute to the solution rather than exaggerate the problem. Whether we are facing a personal, health, or financial issue, an international conflict, or a pandemic such as COVID-19 really doesn't matter. Our response is to live, think, and pray according to God's Word.

Before we delve into Psalm 91, remind yourself that whatever you're facing did not catch God off guard. While it may have surprised you, it wasn't a surprise to Him. Why is it important to remind ourselves of this fact? Because He knew what was coming, and He thoroughly prepared us for it. He prepared not just our survival but our victory. Anxiety and fear shut down our ability to hear, which is central to our experiencing His triumph in the situation. I love to remind myself that the Bible says Jesus was crucified before the foundation of the earth. That means that before Adam and

Eve sinned, Jesus had already provided the answer. He thinks of everything ahead of time, always for His glory and always for our strength. So then, it's impossible for me to face something that He hasn't already thought through with a solution within reach.

Prepared to Make a Difference

Praying the Scriptures has been a highly valued discipline throughout church history. It is the basis for reason and the road map for our interaction with God, which we call prayer. And in this current challenge we must revitalize this practice. Psalm 91 gives us the framework for prayer, personal reflection, confession, decrees, and our redemptive assignment.

This psalm is titled "Safety of Abiding in the Presence of God" in the NKJV. If we learn nothing else through this prayer, the title reveals the real purpose behind it. Safety is the fruit. But the goal is the discovery of, realization of, and delight in the manifested presence of God on His people. I believe His manifest presence on us is the key to divine health—body, soul, and spirit. Learning to host Him, to yield to Him, to cooperate with Him, is what He is training us to do in this particular season.

Every weekend, people all over the world gather in sanctuaries large and small, waiting to hear the teaching of the day. The beauty of the Word of God is what brings us together. The teaching of His Word is vital to our health. But when the Israelites were in the wilderness, they encamped around the tabernacle, which housed the actual presence of God. God was central, and everything else about their lives rotated around their value for the God who was with them. They gathered around the presence.

I look forward to the day when the church gathers around the presence of God again. I do not mean instead of our need to hear preaching and teaching of Scripture. I mean the priority, when we gather, of acknowledging His abiding presence, not just what He has said.

Read through this psalm, and then we'll look at each verse and how it is to affect our thoughts, our prayers, and ultimately our behavior.

Psalm 91

He who dwells in the secret place of the Most High
Shall abide under the shadow of the Almighty.
I will say of the LORD, "He is my refuge and my
        fortress;
My God, in Him I will trust."

Surely He shall deliver you from the snare of the
        fowler
And from the perilous pestilence.
He shall cover you with His feathers,
And under His wings you shall take refuge;

His truth shall be your shield and buckler.
You shall not be afraid of the terror by night,
Nor of the arrow that flies by day,
Nor of the pestilence that walks in darkness,
Nor of the destruction that lays waste at noonday.

A thousand may fall at your side,
And ten thousand at your right hand;
But it shall not come near you.
Only with your eyes shall you look,
And see the reward of the wicked.

Because you have made the LORD, who is my
    refuge,
Even the Most High, your dwelling place,
No evil shall befall you,
Nor shall any plague come near your dwelling;
For He shall give His angels charge over you,
To keep you in all your ways.
In their hands they shall bear you up,
Lest you dash your foot against a stone.
You shall tread upon the lion and the cobra,
The young lion and the serpent you shall trample
    underfoot.

"Because he has set his love upon Me, therefore I
    will deliver him;
I will set him on high, because he has known My
    name.
He shall call upon Me, and I will answer him;
I will be with him in trouble;

I will deliver him and honor him.
With long life I will satisfy him,
And show him My salvation."

—PSALM 91:1–16

The word of God helps us to position our hearts in a way that honors Him. Our faith prompts us to believe that in every hellish situation, Jesus has predetermined to get vindication. He has already decided to reverse any negative effect on the promotion of the gospel. He is always set up to receive the glory and victory.

An Invitation to the Secret Place

The very first verse gives us the key, not just for this psalm but also for the victory it promises.

He who dwells in the secret place of the Most High
shall abide under the shadow of the Almighty.

—PSALM 91:1

The secret place is a dwelling place. It is home, a place of habitation. This is where we find both rest and refueling to fulfill our purpose. Never is it entered to obtain favor with man or somehow to improve our image with others. It really is secret. Never do we enter to let others know we are really devoted to Jesus. It is personal and private. This is where we discover who we are when no one is watching. This dwelling place brings strength, refining, and inspiration for our future. These are the results of walking closely with Jesus.

I believe in the corporate prayer meeting. Sometimes things get accomplished there that would be hard to do on our own. However, we are shaped and built in the secret place. The alone time with Jesus is what dials in our awareness of His presence in our daily lives. Like all things in the kingdom lifestyle, this awareness is continually built as we walk faithfully through the years. This awareness grows over time.

This secret place may be a room in the house. Or it could be a certain time of the day. The focus is alone time with God. And this alone time builds something in me that affects my entire life. It teaches me how not to grieve or quench the Holy Spirit, which is the presence of God in my life. But equally important is learning what I am supposed to do, which is to illustrate the life of Jesus.

So many of us read John 15, where Jesus taught the importance of abiding in Him, but then we walk away clueless as to what He meant or how to do it. And yet it is so important that it is compared to a branch that stays connected to the vine. If it separates, it dies. And if it abides correctly, it not only stays alive but also bears fruit for His glory. Abiding is quite significant indeed.

One of the primary promises of Jesus connected to this subject of abiding—living conscious of the presence of God—is found in John 15:7: "If you abide in Me, and My words abide in you, you will ask what you desire, and it shall be done for you." Being brought into this role of a co-laborer with God is quite significant. Co-laboring is part of our original design, as found in Genesis 1:28. As we abide in Him, His Word becomes the treasure of our hearts and minds, positioning us to pray and see anything happen that concerns us. Abiding in Christ is the ultimate dwelling place, a place from which we do life.

The second half of Psalm 91:1 deals with something that is rarely understood. It says we abide in the shadow of the Almighty. Shadows are dark places. We almost always liken darkness to evil. We correctly call the devil and his demonic realm the powers of darkness. And yet the Scripture teaches us that darkness and light are the same to God. (See Psalm 139:12.) In Psalm 18:11 we find out that darkness is "His secret place." This never means God is influenced by darkness in the sense of evil. It simply means as the sovereign One, nothing escapes His rule. These verses are also saying that God in His mercy veils Himself in darkness because we couldn't handle the brilliance of His light.

This part of verse 1 clarifies something that all of us need to know: sometimes it is so dark around us because God is very near. It's not because we are lost or the devil is in control or anything of that nature. His nearness is what causes things to be out of focus. The shadow of His presence makes it difficult to see well. It's not punishment. Nor is it to point out something that is lacking in our lives. In reality it is a privileged moment where God is drawing very near, not so we'll get some profound strategy for battle, but so we'll draw near to Him. These moments often carry with them an invitation to refine our focus and rediscover what really is important. We are often reduced in these seasons in ways that seem painful, and yet they are some of the most wonderful moments of our lives. And as my son Brian says in his book *When God Becomes Real*, "Consider it a gift when God becomes your only option."[1] These moments are truly a gift from God. Simplicity in our devotion to Christ is more powerful than a thousand great strategies for war. When we affectionately draw near to Him, He often fights for us. (See Isaiah 42:10–13.)

An interesting picture that should affect our perspective on the battles we all face in life is found in Psalm 23:5. This verse says of God, "You prepare a table before me in the presence of my enemies." It's not that the enemy of our souls somehow invaded our alone time with Jesus. Rather, God invaded the moment of the devil's onslaught in our lives and set up a table of intimacy and nourishment in the midst. Stunning! God didn't invade darkness with spiritual guns blazing. He invaded with a table, where we experience His nearness.

That reveals how confident He is in our ability to win whatever conflict we are in.

The place of deepest fellowship with God is sometimes found in the presence of enemies. That means we have a choice to make. Either we keep our eyes on the lover of our souls and fellowship deeply with Him, or we turn our attention toward all that is dark around us and move into fear and anxiety. It looks easy on paper. But in real life, choosing to see Him can be a challenge. The greater your history in the secret place, the easier it becomes to make this choice wisely. I've read two different stories of heroes of the faith who were awakened at night by the devil himself standing next to their beds. On both occasions the men of God looked at him and said, "Oh, it's you." They then rolled over and went back to sleep. That is the confidence that the secret place instills in the life of the believer.

If I am having a romantic dinner with my wife, it's not a time to be looking at my iPhone. It's not a time to be distracted by people at other tables in the restaurant, even if I see people there who I know hate me. My attention must be on my wife. While I may be in view of the enemy, I am not within reach.

In reality my intimacy with God is the greatest threat to the devil. In that place of intimacy is where I am delighting in something he will never have. At that moment, he knows I've chosen love over fear.

It's very critical to the impact and success of our lives that we see how our choices, motivations, thoughts, and ambitions come from one of two places: love or fear. When I choose love over fear, I become positioned to enter more deeply the secret place that He has set aside for me.

Anytime we see the devil at work around us, there's a place of intimacy with God in that setting. Only love can find it. Refusing to fear and turning our affection toward Him enable us to see the divine moment created for us in the middle of something that appears chaotic.

Our Confession Matters

> I will say of the LORD, "He is my refuge and my fortress; my God, in Him I will trust."
>
> —PSALM 91:2

This is a remarkable part of this psalm because it is the first of only two verses that give us something to do. The rest of the psalm reveals His promises and/or His response to our obedience. Verse 2 is the place where we take action.

Historically this type of verse is where I obtain information to use in praise. More specifically I turn these words into something I direct to Him. "God, You are my refuge, my hiding place. I find refuge in You. You are my glorious fortress. And I trust in You entirely!"

That is a very legitimate practice and a very approachable way to view these songs of Scripture. Our praise to Him is vital. But it's important to notice that in this psalm the words were not given in praise directly to God. They were a confession and/or a declaration said to other people. This psalm must be spoken to others.

As I ponder the concept of speaking to one another, I remember this great passage in Ephesians:

> And do not be drunk with wine, in which is dissipation; but be filled with the Spirit, speaking to one another in psalms and hymns and spiritual songs, singing and making melody in your heart to the Lord, giving thanks always for all things to God the Father in the name of our Lord Jesus Christ, submitting to one another in the fear of God.
> —Ephesians 5:18–21

Speaking to one another in psalms, hymns, and spiritual songs is in the context of being filled with the Holy Spirit, living under His influence, with thankfulness and correct relationships of honor toward each other. There's a context for victorious words and songs given to one another.

Perhaps my favorite passage in this regard is found in Isaiah 35:

> Strengthen the weak hands, and make firm the
> feeble knees. Say to those who are fearful-hearted,
> "Be strong, do not fear! Behold, your God will
> come with vengeance, with the recompense of
> God; He will come and save you."
>
> Then the eyes of the blind shall be opened, and
> the ears of the deaf shall be unstopped. Then the
> lame shall leap like a deer, and the tongue of the
> dumb sing. For waters shall burst forth in the wil-
> derness, and streams in the desert.
>
> —ISAIAH 35:3–6

This profound passage describes the result of speaking to one another words of courage and faith. We are to find those who are bound by fear and not make them feel shame or guilt for their fear. Pointing to the problem rarely gets us out of the problem. People are hungry for solutions. It's just that they're often ignorant of solutions, or they've been so discouraged through disappointment that they've lost the courage to pursue them. But that's where we step in to help as a body of believers. Because we are *one*, our choices really do affect others. We must do what we can to make sure each part of the body we're connected to lives with great hope, great vision, and great faith.

Stand with each other in times of weakness, speaking right things to one another, such as, "Be strong, do not fear! Behold, your God will come with vengeance, with the recompense of God; He will come and save you" (v. 4). These are words of faith and courage. They bring or release the hand of God into that person's life.

The passage continues, "Then the eyes of the blind shall be opened." These verses describe the miraculous intervention of God into the impossibilities of people's lives. The part we cannot afford to miss is that the miracles are released as God's response to how we talk to one another.

The conclusion to this extraordinary story is not just a release of miracles to the part of individuals' lives that was hurting. That certainly would have been enough. But the God of abundance goes far beyond the miracle for the individual and brings a complete spiritual awakening to the entire culture. This is what's being addressed with His statement about waters in the wilderness and streams in the desert.

It's also interesting to note, the overwhelming testimony of Scripture is that when God speaks of a spiritual crisis of any kind, His answer is water, which is a symbol for the Holy Spirit. I need only to remind the reader of this reality with Joel's promise of the outpouring of the Holy Spirit in the last days. (See Joel 2:28–32.) This is biblical language for the move of the Holy Spirit.

So then, how did this mighty outpour of the Holy Spirit start? How did this move of God become released into society in such extreme measures that it affected both their wildernesses and their deserts? *The ignition point was what they said to one another.* And that brings us back to this most precious part of Psalm 91, which is, again, the first of only two parts that tell us to do something: "I will say of the LORD, 'He is my refuge and my fortress; my God, in Him I will trust'" (v. 2). Such words focus on His greatness and His value as being trustworthy. This declaration is not an opportunity to exalt one's personal faith. He receives all the glory, again and again.

The Promise of Deliverance

Surely He shall deliver you from the snare of the fowler and from the perilous pestilence.

—PSALM 91:3

Much like the blessing Aaron was to speak over Israel, this psalm is a declaration to be made over the people of God. The end has God's response. Psalm 91 is a confession, a decree, and a prophecy all at the same time.

Blessings are to be spoken, not just thought. They are a genuine part of God's economy; He often uses this method to transfer heavenly resources into our lives. Perhaps it's because it emphasizes our need for relationships whereby we can demonstrate the reality of our love for God. Here is the blessing of Aaron, from

Numbers 6, spoken over the nation of Israel. It can be, and often is, still spoken over the people of God today:

> The LORD bless you and keep you; the LORD
> make His face shine upon you, and be gracious to
> you; the LORD lift up His countenance upon you,
> and give you peace.
>
> —NUMBERS 6:24–26

The "snare of the fowler" in Psalm 91:3 refers to a trap used to catch birds. Sometimes we experience the sting of being caught in a trap we were ignorant of, and we need deliverance. "Perilous pestilence" refers to dangerous disease, including pandemics and plagues. Maybe the outbreak of the novel coronavirus has affected our lives. In response, He promises a swift and effective deliverance.

This basically means no matter where you are in relation to trials, difficulties, or crises, He is there to set you free. He comes to deliver you from the traps that have been set for you by the enemy and from outbreaks of disease that sweep the globe.

Don't misunderstand me: Life is not a simple Christian formula where we do steps one, two, and three and we always have our desired outcome. This life is a relational journey. These situations are always about our relationship with God.

You and I focus on the *outcome* of things—the miracle, the provision, and the protection. God focuses on the *input*—the day-to-day interaction with Him where we learn how to do life. This process is where we are shaped and conformed into the image of Jesus in every part of our lives. In this journey of relationship, everything becomes useful in the hands of the sovereign God, who will be glorified in every situation and impart great strength to all who trust Him.

Hiding in Him

> He shall cover you with His feathers, and under His wings you shall take refuge; His truth shall be your shield and buckler.
>
> —Psalm 91:4

Our place of greatest safety is near His heart, "under His wings." This is the picture given to us in this verse. In this place, we find the value of truth, which becomes our safety. The picture is clear. Truth in this metaphor is a shield that protects us. A buckler is a small shield used in hand-to-hand combat. In Ephesians 6:16 Paul refers to the shield of faith. It's not hard to see the connection between the two. To put it another way, the shield of faith is established in truth.

The bulk of Scripture shows us the nature of courage and our assignment of warfare. We see David pick up stones and run toward Goliath. We see Elijah stand in front of at least 450 demonized false prophets and occultists and challenge them to a contest to see whose god is really God. We read of Moses facing a sea and holding out his staff, only to see the sea part. The point is, from Genesis to Revelation we are provided with examples of courage to aggressively face our enemies and our trials. And sometimes we even run toward them.

So when we come to verses such as Psalm 91:4 that describe hiding and seeking refuge, they might catch us by surprise. Suddenly the courageous ones look for shelter. As we'll find later in this psalm, nothing could be further from the truth. Our strength to run into a battle is found in our intimacy with God in the secret place. Drawing near to His heart is what instills us with the courage to face the challenges set before us.

This reminds me of Isaiah's calling to become a prophet, found in chapter 6 of the book that bears his name. This portion of Scripture describes a terrifying moment for Isaiah. He saw God sitting upon His throne. He saw the seraphim that surrounded the throne, and he heard their decrees. This holy moment caused Isaiah to be completely undone. His own uncleanness became unbearably obvious to him.

He found himself so near to the heart of God that the furthest thing from his mind was his own strength or significance. He was about to learn that sometimes to find your significance, you first have to find your insignificance. He was at that place. And then he heard the voice, the heart of God in verse 8:

> Also I heard the voice of the Lord, saying: "Whom shall I send, and who will go for Us?"
> —Isaiah 6:8

I'm not sure that Isaiah even thought about how to respond, as the question wasn't addressed to him. He was actually overhearing a conversation between the Father, Son, and Holy Spirit. It appears to me that he found himself automatically volunteering for whatever God wanted without reasoning through or analyzing it in any way. That's what happens when you're close to His heart.

Perhaps Isaiah's realization of how unqualified he was in his own strength is what qualified him. In this throne room experience, he discovered his insignificance. And almost strangely he stepped into significance.

We are always undone before we are built up because what God is building will not be added to what we have built. It must be all His. As a result, it's always about the grace of God. It is never anything else. It's not about our vision, our faith, our purity, or any such thing. All those things are useful and necessary in their place. But they are also completely useless without the grace of God.

Not Afraid of the Dark

> You shall not be afraid of the terror by night, nor
> of the arrow that flies by day, nor of the pestilence
> that walks in darkness, nor of the destruction that
> lays waste at noonday.
>
> —Psalm 91:5–6

The foreboding spirit basically causes one to believe that even if things are going well right now, something bad is going to happen. Fear and anxiety work to keep us off balance by compromising our spiritual equilibrium. Scripture tells us that the enemy comes to steal, kill, and destroy, and when we embrace fear, we invite the thief into our homes.

Some say fear is the opposite of faith or the absence of faith. I believe it's more accurate to say that fear is faith in the inferior; it's faith in the lie of the enemy, ultimately leading us to unbelief, which wars against God's truth and His nature of perfect faithfulness. We call this war between God and Satan—between truth and lies, between light and darkness—spiritual warfare.

The biggest area of spiritual warfare is in the mind. By that I don't mean it's in the imagination. It exists in our thought realm, fighting over which reality we will live from. Will it be from the mind of Christ or from the mind of all that is inferior?

Paul described these attacks on our thought life as

fiery darts. Establishing us in the mind of Christ has always been one of God's primary goals for us. This has also become one of our greatest tests. I know the mind of Christ has been given to us, as announced to us by the apostle Paul in 1 Corinthians 2:16. But the challenge here is the same as one I described earlier: there's a difference between what's in my account and what's in my possession. How we think when we face a challenge, problem, crisis, or opportunity reveals how much of the mind of Christ we live with. And if miracles are not a regular part of your thought process, then you're not entirely in the mind of Christ.

Anxiety and fear are not areas of personal difficulty for me. It's not that I've not had to deal with them; they have just not been a stronghold in my life. And yet I must admit, in the last year or so, I've had to battle these issues more than almost any other time in my life—especially at night.

It is true that often we face different types of problems in the night than we do in the day. The enemy wants to rob us of sleep, as that is the time God gives us instruction. He designed sleep for our benefit, as it is there we find recovery and refreshing. When that is taken from us, our daytime lifestyle is affected.

On many nights in the last eighteen months or so, I've had to get up in the middle of the night because my mind was too active to sleep. Often I walked the floors, praying, worshipping, and reading from the promises of God. Other times I simply got up and did mindless activities, such as scanning my social media pages or watching TV until I became sleepy again.

The point is, anxiety will rob you of the lifestyle of rest, which ultimately becomes the lifestyle of faith. Psalm 91:5 addresses this as the "terror by night." If the enemy wins the battle over the night, he has brought about a lessening of your creative influence and clear thinking during the day. Your voice in some measure has been compromised.

Prepare yourself for victorious sleep. Keep away from things that provoke or cause you to be anxious late in the evenings. Schedule time to deal with those kinds of things. Don't ever go to bed mad. Anger works deep into our souls, affecting our inner being. Before getting into bed, shed the things that concern you, and confess your trust in God in all things. Put your concerns into His hands, and rest in the wonder of His promises.

I like to turn my heart of affection toward Him as I lie in bed until I can sense His presence. In that engagement of presence, His and mine, is how I like to go to sleep.

I once had the Lord wake me with His voice. I remember it so clearly. It was a Saturday night, and I was to get up very early for our multiple services on Sunday. I was awakened hearing these words: "He watches over the watch of those who watch the Lord." I spent the rest of the night pondering those words and what He meant for my life.

My conclusion is that we all have many responsibilities. And like a watchman on a wall who is ready to notify the citizens of that city of impending danger, so I, as a husband, dad, granddad, friend, and pastor, have things that I watch over, praying and serving. But in this word He let me know that when I put my attention on Him, He attends to the things that concern me. Perhaps this is a part of what is meant by "Seek first the kingdom of God and His righteousness, and all these things shall be added to you" (Matt. 6:33).

Refusing Fear on the Right and Left

> A thousand may fall at your side, and ten thousand at your right hand; but it shall not come near you. Only with your eyes shall you look, and see the reward of the wicked.
>
> —PSALM 91:7–8

Much like the illustration we have in Psalm 23:5 where we are seated in the midst of our enemies, in Psalm 91:7–8 we have the chance once again to choose not to fear, regardless of what surrounds us. Seeing others fall is not a sign that we will. We must not allow our thinking to go down that hole. It's too hard to climb out. We are not bound by the failures and bad experiences of others. They are not indications of what is coming our way.

Now just imagine what these verses declare! You are surrounded by thousands and thousands of people who all fall. And there you are in their midst, standing upright and strong. That is the result of believing what is written. Regardless of who falls, you stand. This is not the self-confidence expressed by the disciples when they all told Jesus they wouldn't deny Him. This is a confidence in the promises of God that results in a complete and total reliance on His grace.

Verse 8 describes God's judgment on the wicked. There are two extremes here I'd like to avoid. The first extreme is the group that constantly declares that God is going to judge an individual or a people group. Here's an example of what I'm referring to. Several years ago I had a lady come up to me and ask me to agree with her in prayer. I said, "OK. What do you want to pray about?"

She responded that I should agree with her for the judgment of God on the city of San Francisco. I told her there was no way I was going to agree with that prayer. Why? We're still in the season of grace, and I am praying for a mighty move of God in that city He loves. She then tried to cast a demon out of me, which was quite humorous at the moment. After that didn't work, she just left, mad. Looking back, it was also quite sad.

While there's not enough room in this book to deal with this subject adequately, let me just say that our authority is to be used to intercede for people who are bound by sin and can't get out by themselves. It is to be used to speak for those who have no voice, sometimes not knowing their right hand from their left, morally speaking. Misusing that authority is an abuse of our priestly role as believers that none of us will want to have to explain before our Father, who will ask us to give an account of our words.

At the other end of the spectrum is the group that says that all judgments are entirely Old Testament issues. They believe there is no more judgment and no hell. So much of the Scripture, even the New Testament, has to be ignored or explained away to arrive at that conclusion. Oftentimes people embrace either of these two opinions as a reaction to the error of the other extreme.

I consider what Psalm 91:7–8 says about the reward of the wicked to be of paramount importance. Please understand my heart on this subject. I don't want to see anyone judged. My heart is to see the corrupt one repent. I want the biggest pervert on the planet to find the mercy of God. His mercy is designed for the worst of us. My prayers are constantly for the mercy of God to be demonstrated, even on the life of ones most despised by culture and society. His mercy is that great. Now, I also request this of the Lord: "If they absolutely will not repent, then please demonstrate Your judgment in such a way that the fear of God is restored to our world." But for me it's a last-resort measure.

The Results of Abiding

> Because you have made the LORD, who is my refuge, even the Most High, your dwelling place, no evil shall befall you, nor shall any plague come near your dwelling; for He shall give His angels charge over you, to keep you in all your ways. In their hands they shall bear you up, lest you dash your foot against a stone.
>
> —PSALM 91:9–12

The picture in this passage is quite profound. It is basically saying if we abide in God, no evil or plague can enter that dwelling because God is the dwelling/house we live in. Nothing of the powers of darkness can enter His person. I remind you, we are His body on earth. I hope we can learn to enter the reality described in this concept and theologically established in Ephesians 1:22–23: "And He put all things under His feet, and gave Him to be head over all things to the church, which is His body, the fullness of Him who fills all in all."

The angelic realm is more important in our daily lives than probably most, if not all, of us realize. Here is a promise about their care over us. In fact, this is the verse that Satan quoted trying to get Jesus to act outside His character of doing only what the Father is doing. Of course, Jesus said no and then spoke the Word back into the situation to create divine order through the proper use of Scripture. In Luke 10:19 Jesus also taught the basic point of this verse to those who were to follow Him: "Behold, I give you the authority to trample on serpents and scorpions, and over all the power of the enemy, and nothing shall by any means hurt you." It's obvious that God intended us to enjoy the same ministry as Jesus to destroy the works of the evil one. (See 1 John 3:8.)

It is foolish to worship angels. It's equally foolish to ignore them. They came and ministered to Jesus when He needed it. They were used throughout Scripture to protect and/or help people carry out the purposes of God. Hebrews 1:14 says of angels, "Are they not all ministering spirits sent forth to minister for those who will inherit salvation?" We are their assignment. They are there to help us not to stumble and to succeed in fulfilling our purpose.

When time is over and eternity has begun, we will be able to see more clearly how often the angels of God were there to assist us in carrying out our God-given assignment. They also usher the presence of God into a given situation.

Born for Advancement

> You shall tread upon the lion and the cobra, the young lion and the serpent you shall trample underfoot.
>
> —PSALM 91:13

This verse stands out because it's only the second time in this psalm we've been given an assignment. This one tells us what we're to do now that we're protected. This verse describes the purpose of our safety: to help others experience the same. Much like the starving lepers who found an abundance of food in 2 Kings 7:8, so we have been given personal breakthrough and a lifetime of testimonies of God's greatness that position us to do the same for others. In this one verse, Psalm 91:13, the delivered become the deliverers.

In verse 12 the angels are protecting us from striking our foot against a stone. But in this verse the foot that didn't stumble is the one that tramples over the powers of the enemy.

Make no mistake, He delivers us for our good. He longs to set us free. But that's not all there is to His work of deliverance in our lives. As those experiences of liberty take root in our lives, they are to spread throughout society by our witness and example. Here we are, dwelling in God, hidden—not out of view but out of the reach of the evil one. And then we, the sheltered ones, are released to trample on the powers of darkness.

What an extraordinary declaration! Again, from Ephesians 1:22, "He put all things under His feet." All things. Feet are the lowest part of the human body. This is saying the lowest part of His body, which is the church of the living God, tramples over all the powers of darkness. And again, the Scripture affirms this concept with "And the God of peace will crush Satan under your feet shortly" (Rom. 16:20).

We were born for advancement and increase. Setbacks are merely temporary pauses in a life moving forward. Delayed answers are gaining interest. Every loss is temporary, while every victory is eternal. This is our life in Christ, all for His glory.

God's Response

> Because he has set his love upon Me, therefore I will deliver him; I will set him on high, because he has known My name. He shall call upon Me, and I will answer him; I will be with him in trouble; I will deliver him and honor him. With long life I will satisfy him, and show him My salvation.
>
> —Psalm 91:14–16

These final verses of Psalm 91 are God's response to those who have chosen to make His presence their dwelling place, enjoying the pleasure of being near His heart. It's an extraordinary reaction from a perfect heavenly Father, spoken to those whose sole focus is the delight of His heart.

I don't think it's saying there will never be problems. It's not that kind of safety. He said He would be with us in trouble and we'd call upon Him and He'd answer. To keep it practical and real, these statements describe someone who is "in" trouble, thus the cry for help. The point is not that we had a problem; it's that He was with us and He delivered us. The whole thing ends with a long and full life.

I once heard of a minister of the gospel who preached only from Psalm 91. He lived a long and victorious life. Anytime a problem came up, he'd turn to this psalm to see what God wanted him to do or what He had promised him in that trial. I'm not suggesting we do that. But I do want to say that this one psalm is so full that we can feast on it for the rest of our lives and never grow weary of His promises.

We are to be intentional in our approach to life. There should be no question whether we are to advance. We need His help, direction, and protection. But our assignment is to go forward and fulfill the purpose for our lives. And this psalm is there to help us maintain the mind of Christ in the midst of crisis or any such thing. During uncertain times we must remember that these are the days we were born for. We were designed to be a people of answers and breakthrough in the midst of calamities. This is who we are.

Praying the Bible

There is benefit in just praying the scriptures by themselves without any embellishment. I do this often. But I also like praying out of my meditations on a particular passage. What follows is just that: a simple prayer from my meditation on Psalm 91.

Praying Psalm 91
Safety of Abiding in the Presence of God

Father, I thank You for giving me access to Your heart. Your presence is my greatest gift and my ultimate dwelling place. I long to live in such a way that You find pleasure in every word I speak and every action I take. Thank You for calling me to Yourself and helping me to learn how to abide in You. This is my greatest joy. You are my refuge, my place of great strength, and my home. I am strong because of You.

I welcome the moments where mystery is greater in my heart than is my understanding. I know it is because You are near, and it is Your nearness that casts a shadow over me. I welcome the shadow of Your presence. For in it I have found peace.

Help me to always see the table You've prepared for us to sit at together, over and above the distractions of the enemy. I cherish these moments and give You all the praise, for You are great and glorious!

What joy I have found in Your perfect faithfulness. You never lie or deceive in any way. Because of that, You are worthy of all trust. I boast in You. And I will forever boast in You, my God. You are my hiding place, my place of great safety. I trust You! I will always trust You!

You are my deliverance when I deserve it and even when I don't. I am alive entirely because of Your grace. And now I give You thanks ahead of time that should an unbearable trial come my way You have already prepared a way of deliverance for me. Thank You, Father, my perfect heavenly Father. You always hear my cry for help.

Thank You for covering me with Your nearness. I hide in the tenderness of Your embrace. And I boldly declare Your truth protects me from the random ideas that the evil one would introduce to my mind. I embrace Your truth as the priceless treasure that it is. Thank You for protecting me by speaking the shield of truth into my heart.

I confess and declare that no plague will come near my family, as the blood of Jesus covers us completely. And I thank You for assigning angels to us that we might be successful in all that You have assigned us to be and do.

It is a privilege to walk in Your name, in Your authority, trampling the powers of darkness for Your glory. May many others see Your goodness as these powers are openly defeated. And may they be ushered into the kingdom as they come to faith in Jesus, our salvation.

And finally, I give You thanks for the promise of long life, for I have set and reset my love upon You. Over and over again, I confess and declare, "I love You, Most High God! I love You with all my heart, my mind, and my strength! Be glorified in and through me. Amen."

CHAPTER FOUR

RESPONDING IN A KINGDOM WAY

ONE OF THE main goals of my life is to learn the ways of God so deeply that I respond to a situation the same way Jesus would. Most of us can figure out the right way to act in a specific instance, given enough time. But my goal is for my Christlike response to be my reaction—something not thought through.

A number of years ago I had a moment where God brought to mind several stories that illustrated the reaction of the people of God to various kinds of crises and tragedies. It amazed me to see how illogical faith is. Now I know that faith is logical to the renewed mind, but it oftentimes appears to be quite unreasonable to the natural mind. Remembering the details of these stories reveals my biblical knowledge. But that doesn't do me any good unless their response becomes my response. For that to happen, I have to experience a crisis.

Before I get into these three stories, let me establish one extremely important thought before we move into the unusual acts of faith recorded in Scripture. We must begin where God starts.

> When I shut up heaven and there is no rain, or command the locusts to devour the land, or send pestilence among My people, if My people who are called by My name will humble themselves, and pray and seek My face, and turn from their wicked ways, then I will hear from heaven, and will forgive their sin and heal their land.
> —2 CHRONICLES 7:13–14

Natural disasters give all of us a chance to do a reset on our lives. It's like rebooting our computers. I don't believe the present crisis is sent from God, as it is inconsistent with the reset that took place two thousand years ago when Jesus revealed the heart of the Father by exposing and destroying the works of the devil, who came to steal, kill, and destroy. Jesus came to give life. That is the model to be followed since then. Regardless of your point of view, we'd all have to agree that God's heart is to heal the land, but it requires people to turn from every other distraction unto God, completely. We are in a moment of international reset.

I would hope that everyone reading this book would be able to say that you've been walking in purity before the Lord, in what Paul called "the simplicity and purity of devotion to Christ" (2 Cor. 11:3, NASB). Or as Jesus put it in Revelation 2:4, that God would truly be our "first love." If not, this verse is an invitation to get things right with God through confession and repentance and help to bring healing to our land. But if walking in purity and absolute devotion to Jesus is true for us, we still have a responsibility to respond to the invitation of God found in this promise. We pray with the same fervency and focus as if the sins of the land were our sins.

Being in a righteous position before God doesn't remove our need to pray for others. In fact, it adds to the passion, as the beauty of living guilt-free before God should motivate us to pray for others with even more conviction. There is a place in prayer where we repent for the sins of others, often called *identificational repentance.* This is where we identify so closely with the people we are praying for that we confess their sins as though they were our own.

This may sound illegitimate at first, but think of it this way: We often use *intercession* as a term for this kind of prayer. *To intercede* basically means to stand in the shoes of another and plead his or her case as though it were your own. This kind of praying is one of the most vital ways to express true intercession.

We see this of Nehemiah when he came to assist his Jewish brothers in rebuilding the walls of Jerusalem. But before he was granted a leave of absence by the king he served, he cried out with prayers of repentance when he heard of their destitute condition. The whole story is worthy of your review, as it is a template for the moment that we are in. Here is a small portion:

> So it was, when I heard these words, that I sat down and wept, and mourned for many days; I was fasting and praying before the God of heaven.
>
> And I said: "I pray, LORD God of heaven, O great and awesome God, You who keep Your covenant and mercy with those who love You and observe Your commandments, please let Your ear be attentive and Your eyes open, that You may hear the prayer of Your servant which I pray before You now, day and night, for the children of Israel Your servants, and confess the sins of the children of Israel which we have sinned against You. Both my father's house and I have sinned. We have acted very corruptly against You, and have not kept the commandments, the statutes, nor the ordinances which You commanded Your servant Moses."
>
> —NEHEMIAH 1:4–7

This is Nehemiah's response to hearing that his Jewish brethren were unable to rebuild the wall around Jerusalem. The wall was in ruins, an embarrassment to the work of God among His people. He confessed the sins of the people of God as though they were his own. He said, "...which we have sinned." Of course, all of us need forgiveness, "for all have sinned and fall short of the glory of God" (Rom. 3:23). But Nehemiah prays as though the sins of multiple generations were all his.

This is why praying with the woman I mentioned earlier, who wanted me to agree with her for the judgment of San Francisco, would have been so inappropriate. There was no identification with those who are in need. Praying on behalf of others can't be done without humility. Praying for *those* people reveals the most careless posture in ministry: an us-and-them mentality.

We are to pray for God to show His mercy to others in the same way He has shown mercy to us. To lose sight of what we've been forgiven of is dangerous. The us-and-them prayer positions us in an arrogant, self-righteous place that is repulsive to the Lord. We must use our favor before God for the sake of others. In a sense, this is what illustrates that we really see what we've been forgiven of.

Repentance, the Way of the Renewed Mind

Repentance is often illustrated with people weeping over their sins and confessing them before God. I love those kinds of moments. They are raw, real, and transformative. The sorrow over sin has brought about deep and genuine repentance. But as important as that expression is, it is not what the word *repent* actually means. The word means to change the way you think.[1] In light of this illustration, I'd describe it this way: sorrow over sin is expressed in confession so deep and so complete that it changes our perspective on reality. Repentance enables us to think and see from God's view of life. No perspective is more stable.

I need to repent only when I'm thinking outside that standard. In fact, His standard illustrates the renewed mind. So then, walking in repentance is a way of life for those with the renewed mind. This is important as we now look at the unusual responses to calamity, each of which models what the renewed mind looks like.

Kingdom Response Number One: Isaac

This is a very interesting story about Isaac remaining in the land during a famine by God's assignment. He could have gone down to Egypt to care for his family, flocks, and herds. Instead, by the command of the Lord, he stayed:

> *There was a famine in the land*, besides the first famine that was in the days of Abraham. And Isaac went to Abimelech king of the Philistines, in Gerar.
>
> Then the LORD appeared to him and said: "Do not go down to Egypt; live in the land of which I shall tell you. *Dwell in this land*, and *I will be with you and bless you*; for to you and your descendants I give all these lands, and I will perform the oath which I swore to Abraham your father. And I will make your descendants multiply as the stars of heaven; I will give to your descendants all these

lands; and in your seed all the nations of the earth shall be blessed; because Abraham obeyed My voice and kept My charge, My commandments, My statutes, and My laws."

—GENESIS 26:1–5

It's an amazing thing to see that sometimes our assignment from God is to dwell in a land where there's a famine. It reminds me of when the Holy Spirit led Jesus into the wilderness in Luke 4. He may take us to such a location, but it's never for the condition of the world around us to affect us. We are to affect our surroundings.

The Bible tells us that both Abraham and his nephew Lot were righteous. But it clarifies something for us that could help us in this story. It says that "righteous Lot...was oppressed by the filthy conduct of the wicked" (2 Pet. 2:7). Lot was affected by his surroundings in a way that preserved his life but not the lives of those around him. Abraham affected his surroundings and was called the father of faith. We are called to have an effect on our surroundings.

In the story of Isaac he is promised blessing because of the effect of his father, the father of faith. And sometimes obedience means we stay where there's a problem because God has a message that is best demonstrated against the backdrop of difficulty.

There is no evidence of God telling Isaac to do what he did next. I'd like to believe that he did what he did because of his confidence in the overriding promise and purpose of his life.

> Then *Isaac sowed in that land*, and *reaped in the same year a hundredfold*; and the LORD blessed him. The man began to prosper, and continued prospering until he became very prosperous.
> —GENESIS 26:12–13

Isaac planted his crops during the famine. In the natural, that is not the wisest use of seed. Sometimes it's better to save the seed for another season when a healthy crop is more assured. Instead, Isaac sowed in the land and reaped a harvest that was one hundred times greater than normal. It was a supernatural harvest.

Generosity is one of the core values of my life. I've heard this story used to illustrate generosity, simply because of the nature of giving likened unto planting a seed. While it works to illustrate that point very well, that is not what happened in this story. Isaac was sowing into his own future. He was a businessman—a farmer and a rancher with many flocks and herds. He was making an investment into his own business at an illogical time.

It is said that in American history, more millionaires were created per capita during the Great Depression of 1929–1939 than in any other era. Crisis is not a time to retreat. Doing so means we don't understand the way God works. The one exception, of course, is when you hear a word from the Lord to do so. Otherwise, business-people must think in terms of how to make righteous advancement when there are difficulties. I say *righteous* because sometimes crises open a door to take advantage of people in a very dishonorable way. Of course, I'm not encouraging that kind of advancement at all. We often hear of different ones taking advantage of others in these situations. I think it's often called highway robbery.

The part that seems somewhat humorous to me is that the Bible says, "The man began to prosper, and continued prospering until he became very prosperous." God wanted to make sure we got it. It reminds me so much of Ephesians 3:20, where Paul says God can do "exceedingly abundantly above all that we ask or think." Whenever God uses so many similar words to describe the same thing, we had better take notice.

The business of Isaac advanced in supernatural prosperity during a crisis. These are times when all of us need to ask what it looks like to invest in ourselves. I know it sounds self-serving, but it doesn't have to be. If we realized more how God expects us to increase and advance in all situations, we might not be so offended at the thought. Our need for wisdom never becomes more obvious than in times of crisis. Wisdom not only enables us to see the future and invest accordingly but also helps us to be helpful and redemptive in the present.

Sometimes the greatest investment we can make for

our future is to help those in need in the present. We do so simply out of compassion. But the Lord promises blessings for those who help the poor. He says He will repay. (See Psalm 41:1 and Proverbs 19:17, for example.) And His interest rates of return are outrageous: thirty-, sixty-, and hundredfold return. (See Matthew 13:8, 23.)

While I love to see people blessed in all things, my target in using the story of Isaac is not so much that we'll have increase, as important as that is. My target is renewing our way of thinking. The common approach to calamity assumes retreating is wisdom when often it is not. Fear often masquerades as wisdom. Whether you retreat or go forward, make sure it is because you see what the Father is doing, and you are positioning yourself for the blessing He has promised.

Kingdom Response Number Two: Nehemiah/Israel

Nehemiah was grieved to hear of the plight of his fellow Jews, specifically as it pertained to rebuilding the walls of Jerusalem. That rebuilding project had more to do with the esteem and overall purpose for the nation of Israel than it did a simple wall. Because of their sins, they lost control over their own lives and became the captives of another nation. But the time of their captivity was coming to an end, and it was time for God's full restoration. What God was doing affected their *outer world* (temple, houses, and city walls) and their *inner world* (their consciousness of the presence of God and of their identity as the people of God with an eternal purpose).

When the rebuilding of the temple started in the days of Ezra and now the rebuilding of the walls of Jerusalem, the Israelites had already been in captivity many years. They had not yet learned the ways of nobility to be expected of them in the years to come. They had great integrity and focus when they were rebuilding the walls.

> Therefore I positioned men behind the lower parts of the wall, at the openings; and I set the people *according to their families*, with their swords, their spears, and their bows. And I looked, and arose and said to the nobles, to the leaders, and to the rest of the people, "Do not be afraid of them. Remember the Lord, great and awesome, and *fight for your brethren, your sons, your daughters, your wives, and your houses.*"
>
> —NEHEMIAH 4:13–14

Perhaps their emotional connection to their assignment was because they were defending their own personal inheritance. They were fighting for their families. It became personal. But they had not yet learned what it was to face difficulties as a community built by families and a nation built with communities. Seeing the bigger picture is the nature of the kingdom.

> And there was a great outcry of the people and
> their wives against their Jewish brethren. For
> there were those who said, "We, our sons, and our
> daughters are many; therefore let us get grain, that
> we may eat and live."
>
> There were also some who said, "We have
> mortgaged our lands and vineyards and houses,
> that we might buy grain because of the famine."
>
> There were also those who said, "We have bor-
> rowed money for the king's tax on our lands and
> vineyards. Yet now our flesh is as the flesh of our
> brethren, our children as their children; and indeed
> we are forcing our sons and our daughters to be
> slaves, and some of our daughters have been brought
> into slavery. It is not in our power to redeem them,
> for other men have our lands and vineyards."
>
> —NEHEMIAH 5:1–5

When the famine hit, some were more prepared than
others. The ones who had the money were buying the
lands of their fellow Jews. The lands they were selling
were supposed to be their family's inheritance, with the
intention that the property remain in their family trust
forever. They had to sell just to eat to stay alive. Others
were borrowing money from each other and couldn't
afford the exorbitant interest rates. As a result, their
children were being put into slavery, some even being
sold to other nations.

Their response to calamity was much like the nations

around them, who looked for every opportunity for personal gain rather than what was expected from the people of God. They used a crisis to advance against their brethren. While they had a heart for their individual families, they lacked an understanding of who they were as a whole: the family of God. They thought nothing of seeing their own people brought into slavery in order to receive the legal payments they deserved because of their contract of sale or the contract of their loan. The point is, they broke the covenant of God as it pertains to being a people who live together, thrive together, and struggle together.

I'm reminded of Acts 4:32–33 when the people of God were increasing in number greatly. But so was the persecution. Their response was what God intended.

> Now the multitude of those who believed were of one heart and one soul; neither did anyone say that any of the things he possessed was his own, but they had all things in common. And with great power the apostles gave witness to the resurrection of the Lord Jesus. And great grace was upon them all.
>
> —Acts 4:32–33

They had all things in common. No one had lack. This is not Christian communism, as some have suggested. It doesn't work as a law. It works only when it's from compassion and the individual rights and responsibilities are protected.

When Nehemiah heard their outcry, he became very angry. This was no small matter, as is seen in chapter 13, where he actually pulled out some of their hair (v. 25)! He called for a meeting with the leaders who had allowed this to happen.

> And I became very angry when I heard their outcry and these words. After serious thought, I rebuked the nobles and rulers, and said to them, "Each of you is exacting usury from his brother." So I called a great assembly against them. And I said to them, "According to our ability we have redeemed our Jewish brethren who were sold to the nations. Now indeed, will you even sell your brethren? Or should they be sold to us?"
>
> Then they were silenced and found nothing to say. Then I said, "What you are doing is not good. Should you not walk in the fear of our God because of the reproach of the nations, our enemies? I also, with my brethren and my servants, am lending them money and grain. Please, let us stop this usury! Restore now to them, even this day, their lands, their vineyards, their olive groves, and their houses, also a hundredth of the money and the grain, the new wine and the oil, that you have charged them."
>
> —NEHEMIAH 5:6–11

This is really a beautiful story. They were being taught the ways of royalty, the ways of nobility, by one who was a Jew but who served in a foreign king's court. He had to know firsthand how royalty treats royalty. Israel was called to that destiny, and there was no better time to learn than in a crisis. What you learn in calamity will remain in abundance.

They were instructed not to charge interest and to restore what they had "legally" purchased. While purchasing another's inheritance may have been legal, it was not ethical for the family of God. God holds us to a higher standard with one another. "Therefore, as we have opportunity, let us do good to all, especially to those who are of the household of faith" (Gal. 6:10). This certainly doesn't mean we treat unbelievers poorly, as this passage makes clear. But God does add extra emphasis on how we treat those in the household of faith.

Nehemiah used his own money to buy back the slaves they had sold to surrounding nations. In doing so, he established a standard to follow. He had no personal gain in even being their leader. He paid for everything of his own resource. This standard brought shame to them as a nation, as most positioned for personal gain refused to do so.

Here's the bottom line of this unusual story: They had broken covenant as the family of God by their disregard for the well-being of other Jews. They had to repent and restore the possessions they had taken from one another. More importantly they had to have a change in their perspective of who they were and why they were alive. The simple act of restoring the family unit, which is the foundation of any society, became the platform God used to instill in them an understanding of what God values. Only working in conjunction with how God thinks and what He values will bring us into our intended destiny. Because of this you never hear the famine spoken of again.

In times of crisis, give attention to relationships. In a sometimes unusual way, God uses our success there as a measurement of what blessings we can actually handle.

Kingdom Response Number Three: Believers in Antioch

The good news of the gospel of Jesus Christ was first brought to Antioch by believers fleeing the persecution of the church in Jerusalem. Jesus had commissioned His followers to go into the whole world and preach the gospel. Instead, they chose to stay in the comfort of the believing community in that great city. I imagine that God lifted some of the protection they lived under to help motivate them to carry out the mission to spread His good news all over the world. It reminds me of the way God used Pharaoh and his armies to motivate the children of Israel to walk between two walls of water from Egypt into the wilderness.

As the church began to grow, Antioch became a center for missionary activity. As such, they had strong influence of the apostles and prophets, which means they enjoyed the stability brought about by God's foundation being in place. (See Ephesians 2:20.) One of the prophets of the day came with a disturbing word. But their response is one of the most remarkable in the Bible:

> And in these days prophets came from Jerusalem to Antioch. Then one of them, named Agabus, stood up and showed by the Spirit that there was going to be a great famine throughout all the world, which also happened in the days of Claudius Caesar. Then the disciples, each according to his ability, determined to *send relief* to the brethren dwelling in Judea. This they also did, and sent it to the elders by the hands of Barnabas and Saul.
>
> —ACTS 11:27–30

The prophecy announced that the famine was going to affect the entire world. Imagine being in the meeting that day when a trusted prophet announced that difficulty was coming your way. In an entirely different story Joseph interpreted Pharaoh's dream and realized a famine was coming to Egypt. He then instructed Pharaoh to set aside food in preparation for that seven-year season. It's not bad counsel at all. In fact, it's considered wisdom. But the believers in Antioch did something that is either foolish or from the heart of God—and there's no in-between. They took an offering.

I remind you that the famine was coming to the entire world, which means it would be coming to Antioch too. Yet the initial response of the Antioch church was to take an offering to help the believers in Judea. This is extraordinary. Recently I heard someone say that it's not how much money I have in the bank; it's how much seed I have in the ground. That is really true.

In this story, which is in contrast to the story of Isaac at the beginning of this chapter, the seed was their giving. It was generosity. It was not sowing into the future, at least directly. All generosity comes back to us in one form or another. But this was pure giving.

Another part of this story that touches my heart is the fact they gave to believers in Judea. I've heard it said that the church must have been hurting finan-cially in that part of the world. And that may be. The part that I'd rather emphasize for my own life is that they were sowing into the church that first brought them the gospel. In other words, it was a gift of honor.

As believers, we give from three underlying motives:

1. *Compassion.* This is where we give to meet human need. It may be food for a single

mom and her children, it could be giving
to the local food bank, or it could even be
giving for cancer research. The point is, we
are moved with compassion to give because
people are in crisis.

2. *Vision*. This is where our tithes and offer-
ings come from. We give because we
believe in the local church and we support
what is happening in and through that
group of believers. This would include our
support for missionaries or the local rescue
mission, as they help to give new direction
to the people who come to them for help.

3. *Honor*. This is the rarest because we don't
yet understand how royalty lives and
responds to life. But we will. We are a royal
priesthood, and we must learn the ways of
nobility, the ways of royalty. The Queen
of Sheba did this kind of giving when
she brought a gift to Solomon. Solomon
did not need her money at all. It was the
queen who needed to give it. Something
wonderful happened to her as a result of
this approach of giving out honor. Before
she left to return home, Solomon gave her
everything her heart desired.

> Now King Solomon gave the queen of Sheba all she desired, whatever she asked, besides what Solomon had given her according to the *royal generosity*. So she turned and went to her own country, she and her servants.
>
> —1 KINGS 10:13

The phrase I want you to hold to is *royal generosity*. It is the way of royalty to give to meet human need, to give out of vision, but also to give because our hearts long to give honor where it is due. As we grow in our identity, more and more we'll see giving from this place.

I recall a wonderful story of Alexander the Great. As the story goes, a beggar asked him for some alms. Alexander responded by giving him several gold coins. Alexander's assistant asked why he gave him so much, as copper coins would have met his need. This great leader responded, "Copper coins would suit the beggar's need, but gold coins suit Alexander's giving." We give out of who we are.

Giving out of honor comes from our identity in Christ, as kings and priests of His kingdom. It also comes from a place that is secure enough to recognize the greatness of another and respond accordingly. The beautiful conclusion to the story from Antioch is that we never hear of this famine spoken of again. The point is, generosity—specifically giving in honor—can silence the voice of a famine in the most unusual way.

Each of these three stories is unique. One story had people in famine and significant social decline. They had to repent from their foolishness and take practical steps to restore right relationships. This silenced the famine. It became the platform for God's blessing in the next season. The other two needed actions that were completely unreasonable apart from God. In other words, Isaac and the church at Antioch each performed an act of faith. One was to sow into the future with investments, trusting God to bring increase during a famine. The other was to put seed in the ground, so to speak, through generosity, expecting that God would look out for their well-being.

A Final Word About Generosity

Generosity is one of the most essential ways to face any kind of calamity. It includes money but is much bigger. Sometimes it's a smile in a store or a phone call to check on a neighbor. It is to become the way of life, not just a button we turn on and off. On many occasions, I have given a sacrificial gift in crisis; I have led our ministry (Bethel) to do this whenever we're facing financial challenges.

During this pandemic, Beni and I have been paying our trainer who helps us in our weight-training workout. The gym is closed, and he has no income. We're also buying gift cards from restaurants that need help in this crisis. We've been aggressively practicing this during the pandemic.

At Bethel we had to cancel one preacher from speaking to us because of the president's order for no large meetings to be held. We chose to honor his request and canceled all public meetings. So we sent this man a substantial honorarium as though he had been here for the couple of days for which he was scheduled to speak. We sent checks to other ministries that have been a blessing to us for many years because we knew they wouldn't be able to travel, and that is their primary source of income. And we are experiencing the same famine as they are. The point is, generosity is the way of the kingdom, and it is the way of our King. It is our lifestyle. It is seed in the ground we'll want to be able to harvest from in the next crisis.

The Final Chapter

In the final chapter I want to walk you through taking Communion—meeting before the Lord with our families, with friends, or even by ourselves. It is vital to return to the absolutes of the body and blood of Jesus. It is a power meal that works to transform us and impact the world under our influence. Prepare yourselves for this challenge.

CHAPTER FIVE

THE POWER OF COMMUNION IN CRISIS

DRAWING NEAR TO God is our greatest position of strength. This is true, no matter the challenges we face. In pandemics, wars, devastation through natural disasters, or even personal crises, we all need a reminder of the One who died on our behalf. He purchased with His blood on the cross what we could never afford: peace on earth and goodwill toward men (Luke 2:14).

In light of recent world events, I thought it best to end this book with the following description of the power of Communion. Our need to return to the basics is never more apparent than when we are the most challenged in our faith. Embracing these basics provides solid footing for the battle. In this case there isn't a more solid ground to stand on than the death and resurrection of Jesus. It is so central to our lives and to our faith that without it we are completely lost. And with this reality coursing through the veins of our lives, absolutely anything is possible. Jesus set the course for a believing group of followers to rise and demonstrate the wonder and beauty that this gospel provides. We are an army of lovers, armed with His compassion and His power to *re*-present Jesus well. And every step of progress we make testifies that Jesus has risen from the dead.

Paul spoke of partaking of the bread and the cup of the Lord, saying, "For as often as you eat this bread and drink this cup, you proclaim the Lord's death till He comes" (1 Cor. 11:26). When our church participates in Communion, we read this scripture and contemplate the most glorious moment in history where Jesus died on our behalf and rose from the dead with the promise of eternal life for those who believe. When we partake of the bread and cup, we proclaim His death and His return! The quietness of the moment is overshadowed by the shout taking place in the heavenlies as we do what we do to glorify Jesus. He is indeed "the Lamb of God who takes away the sin of the world!" (John 1:29).

In recent days Beni and I have been strongly directed to the beautiful privilege of taking Communion. In fact, Beni recently wrote a book on this subject that has helped many restore to their lives what was so important to the early church. I had the privilege of adding a chapter. It is included below. Read through this chapter, and see where you might be able to adapt the direction set here for the situation you are facing. The wonderful truth is, there is nothing you and I will ever face or ever need, in both time and eternity, that was not provided for in the cross. It was that complete.

> He who did not spare His own Son, but delivered Him up for us all, how shall He not with Him also freely give us all things?
>
> —ROMANS 8:32

Developing the Habit[1]

As I mentioned above, we are taught in the Scriptures that in taking Communion we are *proclaiming the Lord's death until He comes.* (See 1 Corinthians 11:26.) I like to picture *proclaiming* as a bold and confident shout! We are declaring in fullness the redemptive work of Jesus found in the gospel. Every time we take the bread and cup in remembrance, we prophetically proclaim what has already happened, as well as what is to come. Consider this: Communion declares that Jesus died for us and is returning for us.

When people surrender their lives to Jesus, they are born again. In other words, they're saved. We know this teaching from God's Word. But then the Bible also says, "Work out your own salvation with fear and trembling" (Phil. 2:12). The implication is that I am also *being saved.* This doesn't deny what happened to me when I received Christ. It just emphasizes the daily ongoing process of personal transformation. So not only were you once saved, but you are also being saved right now.

The crowning touch to this glorious truth of our salvation comes when we die to meet Him or He returns to take us to heaven. In this coming event we find that we *will be* saved. Our salvation will then be complete. Participating in Communion is a wonderful privilege that declares what I call "the bookends of our salvation" in that it addresses the past and the future. Sharing in the remembrance of the broken body and the shed blood of Jesus also helps us with the present.

The Importance of Thankfulness

The most complete passage on the rite of Communion in the Bible is found in 1 Corinthians 11. In it Paul unwraps the insight given to him through an encounter with Jesus Himself. In verses 23 and 24 he says, "For I received from the Lord that which I also delivered to you: that the Lord Jesus on the same night in which He was betrayed took bread; and when He had given thanks, He broke it and said, 'Take, eat.'" Please picture something powerful—the very night that Jesus was betrayed, He gave thanks. Amid the ultimate betrayal, He gave an offering of thanksgiving. He didn't just tell us to praise Him in hard times; He gave us the ultimate example to follow. In betrayal He gave thanks.

Thankfulness is one of the most vital attributes within the reach of every person alive. If I could prayerfully lay hands on people and impart a thankful heart, without question I would. And I would make that the single greatest focus of my life. An impartation of thankfulness would have the greatest impact on the hearts and minds of people. It would literally change the world as we know it. Thankful people attract breakthrough.

Following the major sporting events such as the football championship, World Series, World Cup, and the like, it has become common to see athletes thank God for enabling them to win. I love to see them boast in God and testify of Him every chance they get. But let's be honest; it's not that challenging to give thanks when you've won. The real prize is when we give Him thanks in the middle of something difficult or wrong. That's where the pearl is formed, so to speak. Pearls are formed through irritation. Whenever we give thanks in the middle of hard things, we are presenting something to Him that is priceless. Jesus did it at His darkest moment—betrayal.

The Importance of Remembrance

In verse 24 Jesus said of the bread, "Take, eat; this is My body which is broken for you." Please listen to what He said. He said, "This is My body." There is an invitation into a kind of reverence with this statement. Verse 25 continues: "In the same manner He also took the cup after supper, saying, 'This cup is the new covenant in My blood. This do, as often as you drink it, in remembrance of Me.'"

It's just like the Lord to give us things to do that position us to remember Him. Making this a ritual or tradition that has lost its meaning is so unnecessary. In our hearts we all have the intention of serving the Lord fully and with complete abandonment. But if you're like me, you probably sometimes go for hours in a day without thinking of Him. We're living from His blessing, from His commission, but there are times in the day that we aren't abiding in that face-to-face privilege that we have with God. We are working faithfully, playing with the kids, or taking care of our daily business. With no condemnation, we can all admit that life gets busy. But in His kindness the Lord gives us tools that help us to bring Him back into our minds.

Scripture establishes the principle of pausing to remember. In the Old Testament the Israelites miraculously crossed a river on dry ground. Once they did, they were instructed to set up a pile of stones at that location. This way every time they passed the place where the miraculous had occurred, the stones would trigger the memory. The goodness of the Lord was brought back to mind. (See Joshua 4:1–24.) The devil wants to control your memories. He wants to influence how you think about your past. He wants to influence your perspective on the reality that's going on around you. And he does so by keeping you focused on things that were disappointing, areas where you failed, or times when you were wronged. The Lord, on the other hand, constantly invites you to return to a redemptive focus where you concern yourself with what God is saying and what God is doing.

Partaking Worthily

Paul gives us a somber warning in verse 27: "Whoever eats this bread or drinks this cup of the Lord in an unworthy manner will be guilty of the body and blood of the Lord." This is an interesting part of Communion. Communion hurts you if you're not saved but advances you if you are. The anointing of God doesn't always have the same effect on people. The presence that brings you peace will sometimes irritate others.

Paul admonishes, "Let a man examine himself, and so let him eat of the bread and drink of the cup" (v. 28). Verse 29 is key for us: "For he who eats and drinks in an unworthy manner eats and drinks judgment to himself, not discerning the Lord's body." Paul is defining what it looks like to eat and to drink in an unworthy manner. None of us are clean enough on our own to be worthy to participate in Communion. Jesus is the one whose blood makes us clean enough to celebrate His broken body and blood. It is His provision for us. But in this context Paul is explaining that judgment has come through a lack of discerning the body.

Remember, when Jesus broke the bread, He said, "This is My body" (v. 24). And Paul said people drink judgment to themselves by not discerning the body correctly. Every time you take Communion and are holding the bread in your hand, you hold something that has value, deserves recognition, and can carry judgment.

When we hold the bread of Communion, we recognize that it is a divine moment. The body in this context is most likely referring to the bread we hold in our hands. But there is also reason to think He is referring to the body of Christ, which is the people of God. Both perspectives have merit and are easy to apply in this setting.

Placing correct value on the bread I hold, believing it is the body of Jesus, has a tremendous impact on the effect of that act. But it could also be said that giving proper esteem to the people of God as the body of Christ also has value in this context. The point is, don't reduce this to a mindless ritual. Think, pray, and give thanks.

Paul goes on to say, "For this reason many are weak and sick among you, and many sleep [or have died]" (v. 30). He is saying there are people in the body of Christ who will go to heaven, but because they did not realize the meaning of what was in their hands, they reduced Communion to a religious ritual. Without realizing it, they removed the tool God had put in their lives to bring divine health. And for that reason, many are weak or sick, and some have even died. Yet presumably, week after week, month after month, the miracle was in their hands. But a wrong perspective cancels out the power of that moment. One book calls this "the meal that heals."[2] Well said.

Healing in Communion

Isaiah 53, the prophetic passage on healing, reads, "Surely He has borne our griefs" (v. 4). The literal word for *griefs* is *sicknesses*.[3] In this passage Isaiah is in fact saying, "Surely He has borne our [sicknesses] and carried our sorrows; yet we esteemed Him stricken, smitten by God, and afflicted." When Jesus died on the cross, the Scripture says He became sin. (See 2 Corinthians 5:21.) And when He became sin and died in our place, the Father's anger and wrath were poured out on Him as He became the very thing that was working to destroy us. He took my place and bore what I deserved. Jesus asked the Father, "Why did You turn Your face from Me? Why did You forsake Me?" (See Matthew 27:46 and Psalm 22:1.) The Father forsook Him because Jesus became sin. He poured out His wrath on His own Son, who had become what was destroying mankind.

The movie *The Passion of the Christ* is probably the clearest pictorial description of the sufferings of Christ available at this moment. It brings to life what Isaiah 53:5 records: "He was wounded for our transgressions, He was bruised for our iniquities; the chastisement for our peace was upon Him, and by His stripes we are healed." When the Scripture is talking about stripes, it is talking about His physical beating. They beat Jesus with a rod, and of course He wore the crown of thorns. But those things were minor compared with being whipped with metal shards tied onto leather straps.

The tradition of the day was to use the whip in cases like this and give specifically thirty-nine lashes. That number was so severe, it actually opened up a person's flesh to his internal organs. The understanding was that forty lashes would kill a man, so they would take him to the edge of death instead.

When we say, "By His stripes we are healed," we're quoting Isaiah 53:5, and we're talking about the beating that Jesus endured. We're talking about the moment when He made a payment for our health and our healing. This part of His suffering was not to make it possible for us to go to heaven. This one, in many ways, is for heaven to come to earth in us. His *blood* paid the price to get us to heaven. But His *stripes* were actually a payment for our pain, suffering, and sicknesses here on earth.

Everybody knows you get a new body in heaven. There's no sickness there, no weeping, no pain, no conflict, no confusion. In heaven everything is wonderful. So it's important to see that this part of His provision is for now. Peter quoted this passage from Isaiah in this way: "by [His] stripes you *were* healed" (1 Pet. 2:24). Notice it is past tense. It has already been accomplished on our behalf.

The body of the broken Savior made a full and complete payment not only for our healing but also for our health—spirit, soul, and body. This is the provision of the Lord, and this is its purpose. Remembering Jesus' broken body in Communion is not just a nice sentimental moment when we give thanks that He died so we could go to heaven. It is all that but a million times more. It's a divine moment.

Let's say somebody gives you a car. This individual has gone to the dealership and paid in cash and tells you, "Just go on down there, give them this card, and they'll give you the car. Everything has been paid for—the taxes are paid, the tank is full of gas, and I've covered insurance for the first five years. Go get your car!" It would be foolish for you to go down there and insist on paying for the car again. Yet many people are trying to pay for their healing that's already been purchased. It's a gift that we all qualify for.

Then how is it that Jesus could heal people during His earthly ministry before He had borne stripes on His body? I look at it as when we went grocery shopping with our whole family when the children were small. The key to sane shopping with young children is the ice cream aisle. We strategically went down the ice cream aisle first and got ice cream for each of the kids before we did any of our shopping. It was amazing how angelic they were with an ice cream cone in their hands. We hadn't paid for that ice cream yet, but neither had we left the store. We would put the wrapper in the cart so the cashier could scan it with the rest of the groceries. We paid for what was already consumed before we left the store. And when Jesus died, He paid for everything that had already been consumed *before He left the store.*

Communion Means War

Beni teaches that Communion is a weapon of war, and I really believe that. This meal is not only an act of celebration but also a military tool of battle. We may not feel as if we are engaging in war, but we do many things—celebrating His kindness and His goodness, delighting in His presence, and giving praise—that all have a military effect on the demonic realm. Psalm 68:1 says, "Let God arise, let His enemies be scattered." When we exalt the Lord, there is an effect on the realms of darkness.

The Lord has given us four different weapons for spiritual warfare: (1) the blood of Jesus (Communion), (2) the Word of God, (3) the name of Jesus, and (4) praise. Those are the four basic weapons that we believers use in our lives to defeat and overcome the assaults the enemy brings against us. None of them are focused on the devil. All of them are focused on the provision of the Lord and the person of the Lord Jesus Christ.

As a church, we're on a journey to learn how to access all God has purchased for us. The blood of Jesus is the legal basis for all victory. The cross of Jesus was so thorough in its victory that everything you will ever need throughout eternity was purchased at this one event. There's no other event in history that was so all-inclusive. A hundred billion years from now, we will still be feeding off what was provided for in the sacrifice of this unblemished Lamb.

Communion and Prayer for Family

I try to take Communion every day. While I'm not always successful, Beni and I have made this a regular part of our daily lives, even when traveling. When we do this in our corporate gatherings, it looks a bit different in that it takes a few minutes of our service. But when I'm alone or with Beni, we like to take a bit more time than is reasonable in our corporate Communion time on a Sunday morning.

Beni and I often take Communion together, but a couple of years ago I got too sick to even take Communion. Beni would sit by my bed and take it for me. We would just sit there together and give thanks to God for His goodness. She would take Communion, we'd hold hands, and we'd pray. We would just thank the Lord for His provision, for healing, for divine health. Our approach to life is to see in completion what Christ accomplished for us, so we make the decree, "By His stripes I *was* healed" (following Peter's example in 1 Peter 2:24).

It's important to remind ourselves as we take Communion that it is because of the sacrifice of the Lamb of God that we are alive, that we are forgiven, that we have hope. I pray this reality over each individual in my family. I pray over Eric and Candace, over Kennedy and Selah. I pray for each of them. I pray for the journey they're on, that God would pour out great wisdom and grace upon them, that He'd fill them with prosperity of spirit, soul, and body.

I pray for Brian and Jenn, and I pray for Haley, Téa, Braden, and Moses. I plead the blood of Jesus over every family member. I pray for Gabe and Leah and for their children, Judah, Diego, Bella, and Cruz. And I pray that God would give each one of my family members a heart to know Him. (See Jeremiah 24:7.) I pray that God would deepen their encounters with Him. I pray that He would visit them in the night and visit them in the day.

In the Old Testament one lamb was sacrificed for the entire household. They didn't sacrifice lambs for each individual; they sacrificed one per household. God designed families to be saved together. It was His idea to have entire family lines dedicated to serving the Lord. In this time of prayer for each family, I confess and declare, "As for me and my house, we will serve the LORD" (Josh. 24:15).

The promise of household salvation carries over into the New Testament. In Acts 16:31–34 the jailer was saved, and soon after his encounter his entire household was converted. This is the standard of the Lord. Don't settle for any other. Don't be impressed with the sin your loved one may be involved in; be impressed with the power of the blood of Jesus.

A wonderful testimony illustrates the power of prayer

for a loved one during Communion. We have friends in another state whose son was in extreme rebellion several years ago. The things that he would do right in front of his mother's face were just terrifying. One Sunday his mother was taking Communion in church, and she thought she should plead the blood of Jesus over her son. She just began to pray, declaring that the blood of Jesus had set him free. About two hours after she got home from church, he called in absolute full repentance for his lifestyle of rebellion. This is it, one lamb per household.

Communion and Prayer for Others

I begin Communion by praying over my family members, but then I move outward. Like a pebble dropped into water, I let the ripples of my prayers move outward. I begin to pray for Kris and Kathy and others who are close to me. I begin to pray for absolute blessing over their families, for the fulfillment of dreams in their lives. After that I move to three other individuals whom I won't mention by name. Three leaders in the body of Christ have worked very hard to oppose what is happening here at Bethel. They have attacked me personally by name in their meetings and books. It has become common for them to attack this church body and our friends in the ministry. Their efforts are very zealous in their attempt to destroy what's happening here.

So I include them in my time with the Lord. When I pray for them, I make sure not to pray at them. I never accuse another person before the Lord. The Bible warns us of the foolishness of accusing a servant to his master. They're not my servants; I have no authority over them. Instead, I hold the blood of Jesus out, and I say, "Lord, I ask that You bless the lives of these men. I ask that You fulfill their dreams, that they see their families in total health, that they see their whole family line serve the Lord. I ask that they live a long life, celebrating Your kindness and Your goodness, that You increase the encounters in their lives, and that they prosper." I pray for each of them by name. And I take this moment to be a friend who prays for those who—for whatever reason—have decided to be enemies. Even if they're misinformed, they're displaying their zeal in serving the Lord, and I honor that.

From there I move on to other friends and ministries, some of whom are much different in their approach to God and life. Supporting them in prayer is a great privilege and a wonderful reminder that we need the whole body of Christ. None of us have it all. We need each other.

I also love to hold the elements of Communion before the Lord and pray for the people nearby. I just plead the blood of Jesus over their lives. I want to encourage you to pick up a similar habit.

Scaring the Enemy

I believe in the power of Communion, and I love to confess over my family that the blood of Jesus sets us free. This confession absolutely terrifies spirits of darkness. I know from personal experience that it's the one thing of which they are absolutely terrified. They know that the blood of Jesus is the dividing line that separates someone the demonic can control from someone they can't touch.

It's not just snacking on grape juice and wafers; it is much, much more. I pray that you would fully realize the effect of what you're doing during Communion. And as you do, I believe the Lord is going to release unusual miracles of healing in your taking of the bread. He is going to release unusual miracles of deliverance to people and family members, some of whom might be a thousand miles away or more, by your taking the juice (representing the blood) and pleading the blood of Jesus over their lives.

Prayer while partaking of Communion is possibly one of the most underrated prayers that you could ever pray. Communion is not a magic formula. It's being convinced that the blood of Jesus sets people free. And that expression of faith positions you to influence the destinies of your family, the people around you, and the entire world.

Communion in Crisis

As we face crises, whether personal or global, it's vital to return to our place of clarity and absolute authority. And that is the death and resurrection of Jesus. The broken body and shed blood testify to the lengths God was willing to go for us to see His heart fulfilled in us. Hold the bread and the cup before the Lord, and remind Him of His word to extend mercy for those who seek Him first. Remind Him of His promise that we would see all the nations impacted by the beauty of the gospel.

> All the ends of the world shall remember and turn to the LORD, and all the families of the nations shall worship before You. For the kingdom is the LORD's, and He rules over the nations.
>
> —PSALM 22:27–28

And finally, as you pray over people, whether they are leaders of nations or the nations themselves, come to realize that there is no problem you're praying for that Jesus did not take care of at the cross. It was that sufficient and that complete.

Every attack of the enemy is intended to distract us from the single greatest reality in our lives: the love of God for us. For us to live unconscious of this greatest reality is to live aware of too many other things, each of them inferior. Paul picked up on this and addressed it aggressively in Romans:

> Yet in all these things we are more than conquerors through Him who loved us. For I am persuaded that neither death nor life, nor angels nor principalities nor powers, nor things present nor things to come, nor height nor depth, nor any other created thing, shall be able to separate us from the love of God which is in Christ Jesus our Lord.
>
> —ROMANS 8:37–39

Pray these verses. Confess them, saying, "I am more than a conqueror! This is my life, my identity, and my assignment." Anytime we come into a place of great confidence in praying over our own lives, we've been moved into a place where we can pray and declare effectively over others, even nations. Do so with the absolute confidence that God has assigned us to be alive *for such a time as this.*

PRAYER OF REPENTANCE

If you have read through this book but realize you've never had a personal relationship with Jesus Christ, please pray the following in faith:

Father God,

I believe that Jesus Christ died for my sins and was raised from the dead that I might live forever. I come to You in need of forgiveness. Please forgive me for all my sins. I turn my life completely over to You. Thank You for showing me my need of a savior. I ask You now to be my Lord, my Master, my Savior. I turn from my ways of sin to follow Jesus completely. Thank You for forgiving me, and I now receive the free gift of salvation. Amen.

NOTES

Chapter 1

1. Studylight.org, s.v. "*elpízō*," accessed April 21, 2020, https://www.studylight.org/lexicons/greek/1679.html.
2. Studylight.org, s.v. "*hagah*," accessed April 21, 2020, https://www.studylight.org/lexicons/hebrew/1897.html.

Chapter 2

1. Bible Hub, s.v. "*sozo*," accessed April 21, 2020, https://biblehub.com/greek/4982.htm.
2. Studylight.org, s.v., "*teleióō*," accessed April 21, 2020, https://www.studylight.org/desk/interlinear.cgi?ref=58002022.

Chapter 3

1. Brian Johnson, *When God Becomes Real* (Redding, CA: Bethel Book Publishing, 2019), 158.

Chapter 4

1. Bible Hub, s.v. "*metanoeó*," accessed April 23, 2020, https://biblehub.com/greek/3340.htm.

Chapter 5

1. The remainder of chapter 5 is adapted from Beni Johnson with Bill Johnson, *The Power of Communion* (Shippensburg, PA: Destiny Image, 2019), 147–165. Used by permission.
2. Perry Stone, *The Meal That Heals: Enjoying Intimate, Daily Communion With God* (Lake Mary, FL: Charisma House, 2008).
3. Blue Letter Bible, s.v. *"choliy,"* accessed April 23, 2020, https://www.blueletterbible.org/lang/lexicon/lexicon.cfm?Strongs=H2483&t=NKJV.